TABLE OF CONTENTS

INTRODUCTION

The task of writing a treatise on an art as comprehensive as "palm-reading" is a heavy responsibility, and not one to be approached lightly. Before I embarking on my mission, I shall try to explain what brought me to the doorstep of this fascinating world, and recall my first steps inside it. By doing so I hope to give readers the chance to find the keys which, in a simple and practical way, will unlock the door to knowledge of the human mind.

Most textbooks on the subject offer vast amounts of data and are full of very reliable engravings and drawings. Yet apart from the odd exception, readers usually find such texts heavy reading. They soon feel trapped like a fly in a spider's web, and end up skipping from one chapter to the next, searching for an enlightening word or sentence that will help them untangle themselves.

These treatises have also prompted two very different trends: whereas some authors refer to the subject as "chiromancy", and claim that it is a divinatory art that dates back to the dawn of mankind, others refer to it as "chirology" and regard it to be a perfectly demonstrable science, with origins that lie closer to our own times. Moreover, chirologists mainly purport to define people's characters, and how likely they are to suffer physical disorders or deficiencies, on the basis of statistical data gathered from palm-prints. They deny that it is possible to discover events that are related to our future.

Nowadays this gap between the two trends can be bridged, because palmistry is a creative art and we should not limit or pigeonhole it by trying to give it a definition. Just as our hands have many skills and uses, so palmistry can be interpreted in many ways.

We have always looked upon palmists as interpreters. In fact, from the very instant we are born we do no more than to interpret the world around us, the circumstances that we have to live, the situations that we face and our own sensations, thoughts or feelings. It is the human being's capacity to interpret that lets us embark on the adventure of reading our hands, in the same natural way that we decipher the words of a conversation or on the pages of a book.

I am sure that as you read this book, your interest will grow steadily as you come across the keys to Man's first language: mental language. My wish is that when you reach the last page of the book you will feel ready to practise this art.

THE HISTORY OF CHIROLOGY

Chirology is one of the most ancient sciences of observation, and its knowledge is the result of the discoveries that have been handed down to us over the years.

In ancient times it was considered a form of magic and was known as Chiromancy, because the Greek term *quiro* means hand and *mancia*, divination or reading. So in those days the art could have been defined as "predicting the future and analyzing a person's character by observing their hands".

Later on the word *mancia* was replaced by *logia*, which means science, to give it a more scientific and up-to-date dimension, and also to take it closer to its real nature, because this is an art that involves observation. There is no room here for divination, because instead it interprets the mental messages that are reflected in our hands (fig. 0.1). Moreover, any knowledge is gained by examining and studying the characteristics of the hand, so anyone can study its principles.

We are told that the first hand studies date back to 3,000 B.C., possibly in China. Yet the first written documents are to be found in Indian literature from the year 2,000 B.C. The first reference to chiromancy appears in the *Laws of Manu*, one of the sacred Hindu scriptures that are known as The Vedas.

In Greece, in the 4th century B.C., the famous doctor Hippocrates observed that all of his patients who had heart or lung ailments had thick fingertips or swollen nails, and this discovery gave rise to the present-day term "hippocratic fingers" (fig. 0.2).

Aristotle is thought to have taken a keen interest in chiromancy, and his book *Chiromantia* is regarded as one of the oldest treatises on the subject. He is also reputed to have been the author of several specialized works on the hands and, specifically, one that was written for Alexander the Great, who was very interested in this science.

The Greek philosopher Anaxagoras firmly believed in the veracity of all that our hands reveal, to the extent that he declared: "Man thinks with his hands". Other figures such as Artemidorus of Ephesus, Claudius Ptolomeus,

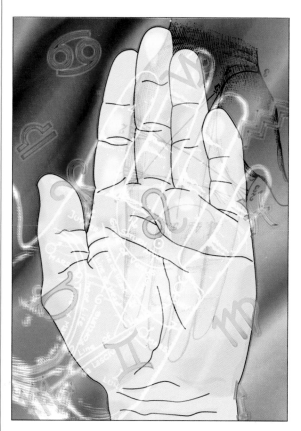

■ *Fig. 0.1. According to chirology, the hand reflects our mental messages.*

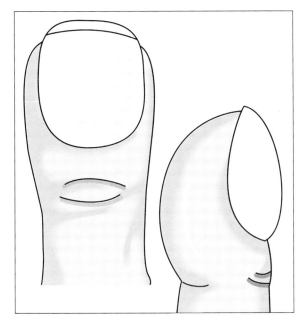

■ *Fig. 0.2. Hippocratic fingers.*

Socrates, Galen, Plato or even Julius Caesar himself were fervent followers of this practice.

Although references are none too clear, many authors suggest that several verses of the Bible relate the hand to thoughts and desires of God; without wishing to spark off a controversy, I shall quote two verses that are worth bearing in mind:

> "Long life is in her right hand;in her left hand are riches and honour"
>
> *Proverbs 3:16*

> "When I put forth my hand against the Egyptians and bring out the Israelites out from them, then Egypt will know that I am the Lord".
>
> *Exodus 7:5*

In the Middle Ages, figures of such standing as Paracelsus and Robert Fludd, well-known specialists in the occult, wrote works on chiromancy.

In the 16th and 17th centuries, numerous texts and manuals were published throughout Europe. Yet the foundations of modern chirology emerged in the 19th century with Cheiro, Benham and Heron-Allen. At the turn of this century, chiromancy enjoyed a strong following in London and in certain circles it was deemed quite normal to consult a palmist. For this reason a group of practising chirologists founded the English Chirological and sought to raise the status of hand-reading to scientific research.

Well into the 20th century, a valuable contribution to the cause was made by Noel Jaquin, founder of the Society for the Study of Physiological Patterns and discoverer of the relationship that exists between organic illnesses and perturbations of the sequence in the pattern of fingerprints. Another valuable contribution was made by Julius Spier, who encouraged Dr. Charlotte Wolf to conduct studies into subnormality though the hands; her book, *The Human Hand*, lists all the examinations that can help to discover hereditary disorders, taking the fingerprints of the newly-born and looking for signs that reveal these possible illnesses before they appear.

GESTURES OF THE HAND

According to certain authors, the hand is faster than the eye and more expressive than the tongue. That is probably why primitive man used sign language before using words. Hand movements are thrifty and can be made faster than spoken language. They are so easy to learn that deaf-and-dumb children quickly make up their own system of communication if they are not taught a pre-established system. Moreover, there are up to seven hundred thousand possible signs.

Nowadays we still use this type of langua-

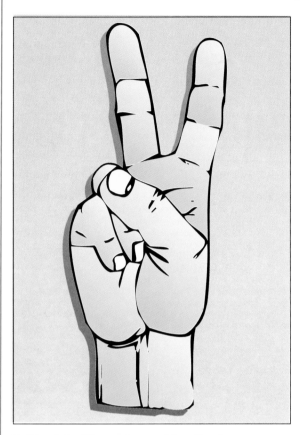

■ *Fig. 0.3. Victory sign used by all cultures to stress the size of the victory.*

ge whenever we run up against the difficulty of a foreign language. It is also still used in sacred practices of religions all over the world, in magic operations, in blessings, invocations, purifications or praying positions. Likewise it is the main instrument for healers, quack doctors and anyone else who cures by laying their hands on people.

If we stop to think just how important gestures are in human communication, there is no denying its relationship with chirology. For instance, we could attempt to analyze the different hand postures one sees in painting's masterpieces, and interpret the messages that their authors are trying to convey to us in their paintings. If you look at Leonardo da Vinci's enigmatic painting, the *Mona Lisa*, you will realize that you cannot see the whole of the famous lady's left hand, which is in her lap, because she is partly covering and holding it with her right hand. If we bear in mind that our left hand represents our past, then the Mona Lisa seems to want to keep her identity a secret. Indeed, some people believe that this odd-smiling woman was Monna Lisa Gherardini, wife of Francisco del Giocondo, Chancellor of Florence. Yet many other people think that it was one of Leonardo's pupils, a transvestite, to whom Leonardo had taken a special liking.

Let's us now take a look at some universal gestures in the light of chirology. We will only analyze a few because Man uses so many that any attempt at studying all of them would be an impossible venture.

One very well-known gesture is the "victory sign" (fig. 0.3) that we use to show that we have successfully attained our goal. We form the sign by holding up our index and middle finger, using our thumb to hold down our other fingers in our palm. If we hold up our index finger, which expresses our personality, and form a "V" shape with our middle finger (or the finger that indicates time), we are saying that it is time we got the prize that our ego deserves. It also suggests that we have won a victory, because we have managed to achieve a balance between our ambition and pride, and convenience, responsibility and introspection.

We form the "power gesture" (fig. 0.4) by closing our fist with the thumb pointing up; an upward-pointing thumb is a sign that we approve an action or a certain fact. But if we turn our fist upside down, and the thumb points downwards, it means that we disapprove of that action. Roman emperors used this gesture in the amphitheatres to spare the life of gladiator who had lost their fight but

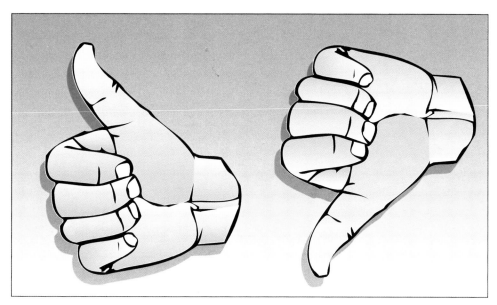

sonality. Therefore it is the ideal finger for pointing at someone or something, or for accusing.

To make the supposed "gesture of agreement" (fig. 0.6) we open our hand and form a circle by joining the tips of our thumb and middle finger. We use this

had fought bravely. An emperor could also have the losing gladiator killed by pointing his thumb downwards. If our thumb represents our "will", by making this gesture we are indicating our approval or disapproval of other people's actions, and what we would do if we were in their place.

We form the "pointing gesture" (fig. 0.5) by closing our fist and pointing with our index finger at the object that we want to point out. This gesture is not only used for pointing out something but also for accusing, above all when we want to report someone's bad conduct. In this case, once again the protagonist is Jupiter's finger, which represents justice, pride, ambition and each individual's per-

gesture to show that we fully agree with the situation or subject that we are being asked about. This is the circle, zero, infinity, the beginning and the end, and it means that we approve it wholeheartedly. However, to form a zero we use our thumb to symbolize our will, and our middle finger to indicate balan-

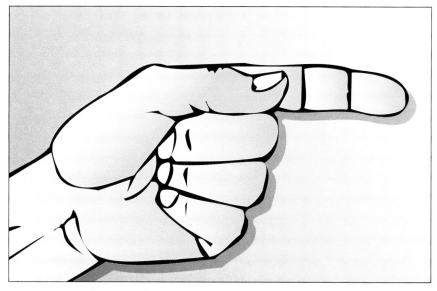

■ *Fig. 0.5. The commonly-used gesture of pointing or accusing.*

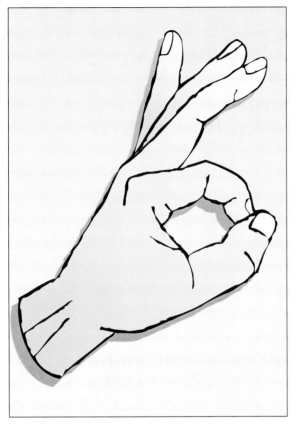

■ *Fig. 0.6. Gesture used to approve a situation or subject.*

ce and timelessness. So not only do we agree at that point in time, but forever.

The "scissor gesture" (fig. 0.7) is a sign that we use to interrupt a conversation or to stop someone from doing something. We use the index and middle fingers, joining them and separating them as if they were the blades of a pair of scissors. When we use these fingers we are trying to tell someone that before they carry on with what they are doing, they should

look for harmony within themselves, because their ideas are misleading and contradictory, clashing with each other just as Jupiter and Saturn fight each other.

Even so, the most frequent gesture among human beings is the hand-shake, which we use to greet each other. Some people say that this greeting first began to be used in the Middle Ages, as a way of showing that you were not hiding a dagger in your right hand, and that you were a friend. Nowadays we shake hands to show another person our intentions. A weak handshake is a sign of selfishness, a desire to save energy. If someone shakes your hand so strongly that it hurts, and they move their whole arm while doing so, it is a sign of an urge to possess. People who behave in this way want to frighten and overshadow their counterpart; but deep down they are scared of making new friends. A normal, balanced person gives a strong yet pleasant shake, without crushing the other person's fingers.

Of course there are lots of other signs that we use very often. If we learn what each finger represents and means, we will see how the messages coincide.

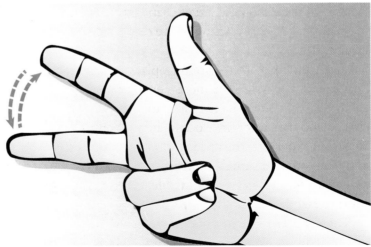

■ *Fig. 0.7. We cut the air with our fingers as if we wanted to interrupt our opponent's ideas.*

CHAPTER I

THE IMPORTANCE OF CONNECTIONS

Scientists have demonstrated that the entire universe is made up of energy, though this energy may take different forms. We know that matter is formed by small particles called molecules, and that in turn molecules are formed by other much smaller units called atoms. It has been shown that the energy in the core of these atoms is larger than any other known type of energy, and now we call it atomic energy.

This principle and system applies to all forms of matter, from the most elementary to the most complex. So the human being is energy, and if an imbalance occurs in our body, either due to an excess or lack of energy, the body issues alarm signals, warning us and forcing us to solve it as fast as possible unless we want to fall ill.

These imbalances are not only caused by physical factors (atmospheric aggressions, environmental attacks, etc.) But also by mental, emotional or spiritual conflicts. Logically, each cause has its own form of expressing itself and gives out different signals.

If our body is formed by three cell structures that match three different forms of the same energy, any conflict that upsets the balance will be reflected by or match one of these structures. Following this line of reasoning, we will analyze three types of structures:

- Dense matter or hard tissues (bones).
- Less dense matter or soft tissues (flesh, muscles, internal organs, viscera, nerves and skin).
- Liquid matter or fluids (blood, water and lymphs).

Hard tissues - The skeleton is the structure of our organism; it is the frame of our body and acts as a foundation for our cellular mass, like the rocks and minerals that underlie the soil on Earth. It is the initial pattern of the final life form that one sees on the outside. It is the densest matter of all our tissues (fig. I.1)

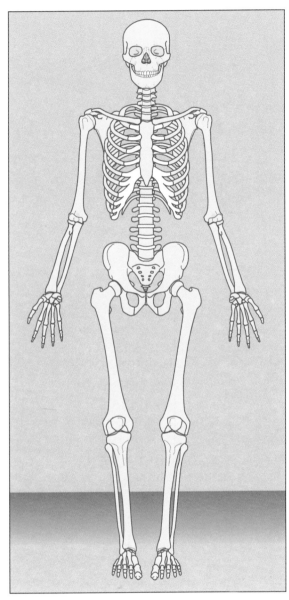

■ *Fig. I.1. Our skeleton is the most dense and energetic matter in our body.*

matter, our point of departure, our source of energy.

Soft tissues - Our flesh, skin, muscles, tendons and ligaments (fig. I.2) are the elements that protect and move our bones, and make them strong and flexible. Our body functions are run by our internal organs, which in turn are operated by the nervous system.

These tissues let our bone system move, just as our mind lets us move, change and transform our interior. And while the soft tissues faithfully protect the energy inside us, allowing it to move, they can also stop it, block it and even enclose it. When we say that someone is prone to depressions because he walks with drooped shoulders, his head down and a bent back, or that someone who walks upright, with a straight back and upright head has no psychological problems,

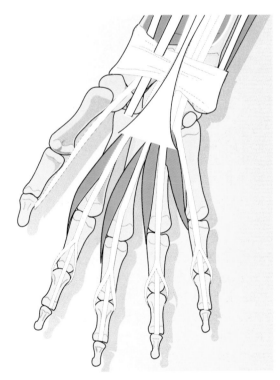

■ *Fig. I.2. Detail of the tendons in the hands. Flexible or soft tissues.*

If we consider that a diamond is the most compact element of the universe, where atom particles move fastest and where there is most atomic energy, our bones must contain the largest amount of condensed energy in our body.

Our bone tissue is the first to form and the last to fall apart; it is our first contact with

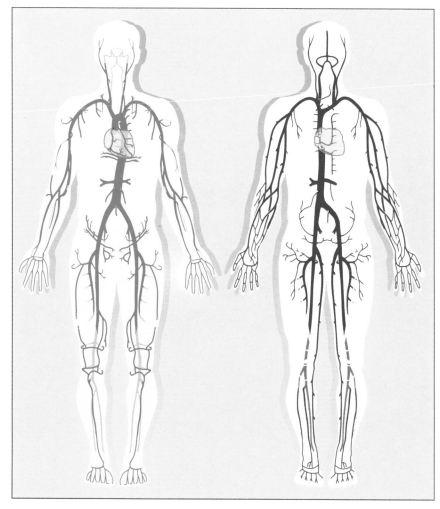

is to carry food and oxygen to all the cells, and remove any impurities, cleaning our organism and defending it against foreign bodies. While the soft tissues let us move, the fluids gives us the sense of direction that we need to move. The fluids match our feelings and, in the words of Robert St. John, we could say that "the hardening of the arteries may reveal a rigid attitude towards free movement of feelings"; that is why the fluids match our emotions (fig. I.3).

LOCOMOTIVE CENTRE

■ *Fig. I.3. The role that fluids play in the body matches the role that feelings play in the pyschological context of the individual.*

we our basing our opinion on this connection.

The soft tissues match our thoughts, which in turn affect the tissues by affecting their function and even changing their structures. That is why we can "read" someone's life experiences by reading the signs on their body, rather like telling the age of a tree by counting the rings in its trunk.

Fluids - 90% of our body is formed by fluids that act inside us as rivers, seas and oceans, just as water does on Earth. Their mission

On the other hand, if we divide our body into the head, trunk and extremities, our thought function is located in our head. It is our head that receives ideas and thoughts from the outside world. After interpreting and analyzing them, and absorbing what interests us, we pass on our conclusions to others. It is also this part of the body that houses the communications centre where we issue and receive, through our five senses, the information we need in order to act in our inner and outer world.

We get our capacity to act from our spinal column, trunk, shoulders, arms and hands; we can put into practice what we have planned in our brain, we can pick up and hold things, embrace, feel and give our mind an accurate sense of dimension and space.

The locomotive centre, which runs from the pelvic zone to the feet, it the system that lets us move and act as we please in the world that surrounds us.

HAND-BRAIN RELATIONSHIP

As we have already seen in this chapter, and without straying from the strictly scientific arena, there is a hidden reality that forces us to admit that every part of our body plays a specific and necessary role, without thereby losing its participation in or connection to the other parts, or to the Universe that contains them.

The fact that we might not want or not know how to interpret all the events that occur around us does not mean that there is message in them; on the contrary, any of the circumstances around us is a material reflection of the great truth that we could discover both inside and outside ourselves. Yet there is no need to exhaust ourselves by trying to interpret our whole environment. Instead we can specialize in interpreting a very small part, such as our hands, which will teach us much more than we had imagined.

To start with, we can apply these connections to our hands, and the bones in our hands will give us an idea of our energy capacity, the mounts will tell us what we think, and the veins that run through them about the feelings that inundate us. But hand-reading involves more than just giving our patients a description of their psychological profile or a more or less accurate definition of their current state of fortune. It offers much more, it reaches the innermost corners of our mind

and opens all the inner doors of our subconscious; it is strong enough to read our real essence and not the image we give other people, which is often disguised by words that fail to express our real feelings.

If we talk about the subconscious we could quote countless theories, because for science our mind remains the great unknown; nevertheless, the theory that is best reflected in our hands is that of a mind that knows no space or time, none of the limitations with which our consciousness confines us; a mind that has the keys to the past, present and future, as if it were a perfect computer that will give us the information we want if we type in the right code.

This idea could make us believe that our fate cannot be changed; that we must live events that are foreseen at birth, with no chance of rebelling. Nothing could be further from

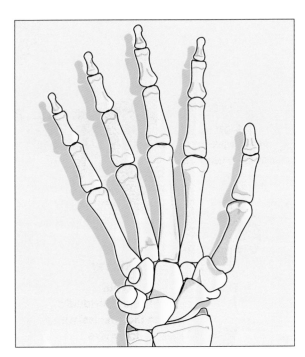

■ *Fig. I.4. The hand is formed by 27 little bones that are joined to each other and contain a large amount of energy.*

the truth. We are free to choose the fate that we fancy from a wide spectrum of possibilities. Yet it is true that our subconscious contains a file with each and every one of these possibilities. Herein lies the power of the human being, the magic responsibility that sets us apart from other living species: the freedom to create, change and transform our environment and fate, albeit within natural laws that have been laid down by the superior force of which we all form part: energy. Now let's return to the idea of connections, this time to look at the hand-brain relationship and see why hand-reading is such a reliable method. We should remember that when we are born, the surface of our brain has not formed com-

pletely, and our hands can only move a little and makes clumsy gestures. Yet when they are six months old, babies start to want to grasp the objects we offer them or that they see around them. It is said that this is when the surface of our brain is fully formed. The nimbler our hands become, the more our brain improves and the faster we evolve psychologically.

This relationship lasts throughout our life; our hands search around for information to feed to our brain, and if there is any problem in our brain, our hands will make it worse by becoming clumsier and less active, to the extent that some psychologists have discovered that they can cure stuttering by forcing

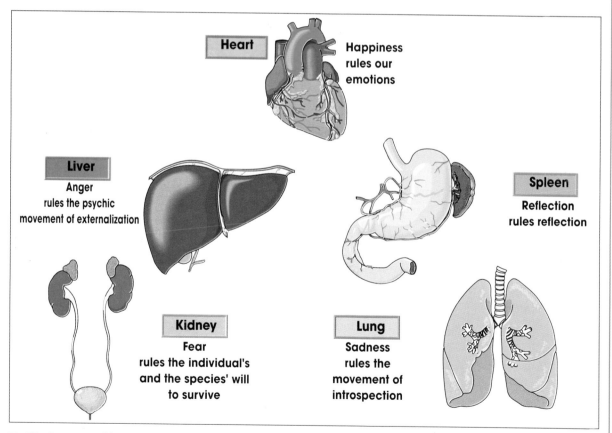

■ *Fig. I.5. In addition to performing a specific fucntion such as breathing, purifying, circulating the blood, etc., the five vital organs (heart, spleen, lung, kidney and liver) produce a given psychic essence.*

their patients to write with their least active hand.

The hand benefits and occupies more space in the brain that all the rest of the body, because the thumb alone occupies ten times more space than our whole foot. Anaxagoras once said that "the brain, helped by the hand, has made Mankind". Should this be true, then everything that goes on in our brain is reflected in our hands, and they are such a perfect match that they could provide the code that we mentioned before. This is the most complex computer known to Mankind: our brain.

As well as serving us, hands also create us. With their 27 small bones (fig. I.4), muscles and mesh of nerves, they have managed to create devices and machines that make our life easier and less painful and also weapons. They can carry heavy loads, hit and even break bricks and just as skilfully play the piano at breathtaking speed, playing hundreds of musical notes in a single minute, perform complex surgical operations or turn out exquisite works of art.

THE CHINESE CONNETIONS

The Chinese discovered these bodily connections centuries ago and ap-plied them in psychology and medicine. Even today we find it hard to believe that they could have reached such accurate conclusions so long ago. According to the principles of Chinese acupuncture, our body is covered by 133 channels called meridians which distribute energy throughout the body.

Considered as a flux, this energy has positive and negative poles (yin and yang), just like electricity does. Five organs are responsible for absorbing and pushing the energy through the meridians; and when handled correctly the energy can be used to cure illnesses or relieve pain, by inserting needles in specific points of our body.

However, the five vital organs - heart, spleen, lung, kidney and liver - not only perform their own functions; they also manufacture a psychic essence called humour, and which is different for each organ (fig. 1.5). Since this essence also circulates through the meridians, the end of its journey is the heart. Here the five essences or fundamental emotions come together to form the individual's real psychic essence which, when sent to our brain, influences our behaviour and shapes our temperament.

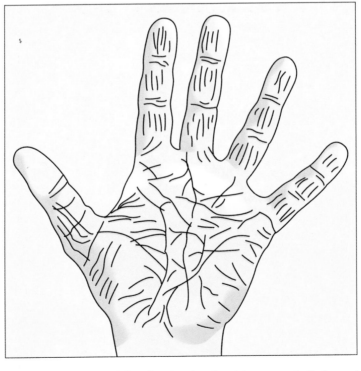

■ *Fig. I.6. A wood hand is hardened, with not much flesh, and joints that resemble the knots of a tree.*

Westerners believe that everything is organized in the brain, whereas the Chi-nese believe that the "conductor" of behaviour is the heart, so allegorically they call it "emperor" and give it authority to govern their emotions. The heart sends the brain the elements that it needs in order to act as the command centre for the whole human body.

The spleen-pancreas rules reflection, which is why Chinese doctors say that too much worry can damage the spleen. The lung governs introspection and its humour is sadness. The kidney rules the individual's, and the whole species' will to survive, so its humour is fear; and too much fear can lead to madness. The liver guides the movement of externalization. Too much activity in the liver can prompt choleric behaviour; yet too little makes one timid, suffer anxiety and lack self-confidence.

To summarize, we could say that psychic activity cannot be separated from organic activity, and that a malfunction of our organs produces a change in our behaviour; and vice-versa, a wrong psychic tendency will upset the function of its respective organ. According to Chinese texts, happiness balances the circulation of energy, anger inverts the direction of energy, sorrow damages our heart's energy, sadness may damage our lungs and fear empties our body of all energy.

In the 20th century, Western medicine is increasingly using the term "psychosomatic illness" to define the psychic, emotional and affective origins of organic or functional disorders.

Different types of hand

Within the context of these connections, the Chinese valued the important role that our hands play in letting us detect illnesses and discover everyone's real personality. By comparing each person's inherited genetic structure, the vulnerability of each organ and the five primary elements into which matter was divided, they classified the hands into five different types that allowed them at a glance to ascertain the patient's psychological profile.

We will now briefly describe the characteristics of each of these types of hand:

The wood hand (fig. 1.6) - The joints of the phalanxes seem hardened, have little flesh and tree-like knuckles; there are numerous deep grooves in the palm and fingers, and the fingernails are either very solid or very fragile.

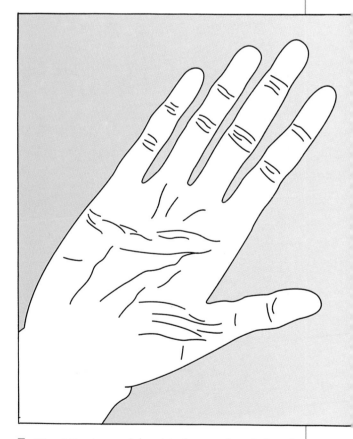

■ *Fig. 1.7. A metal hand is long and oval-shaped, with a narrow palm and long, smooth fingers.*

People with this constitution suffer a natural weakness in their liver, bile duct and the corresponding meridians.

The metal hand (fig. 1.7) - Long, oval, with a narrow palm and long, smooth and tight fingers. The skin is dry, rough and may turn purplish because the individual is very vulnerable to the cold and so may suffer chilblains. There are three folds in the joints between the phalanxes. People with this type of hand suffer lung or intestine trouble and skin diseases.

The fire hand (fig. 1.8) - This hand is also long but the fingers are longer than the palm. The fingers are slender, nimble and full of life, and can be separated from one another. It is a reddish hand, very elegant and delicate. People with this type of hand suffer a natural weakness in the heart, small intestine and the respective meridians.

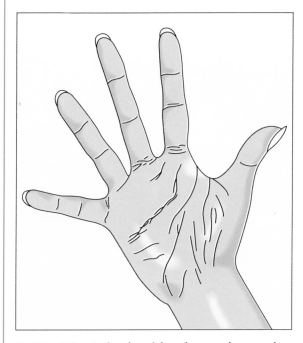

■ *Fig. I.8. A fire hand has fingers that are longer than the palm, sharp and nimble and easy to spread.*

The water hand (fig. 1.9) - Spatular and short, with a soft, swollen palm and fingers, and a blackish hue, especially in the knuckles. Its soft fingernails curve towards the flesh of the fingers and resemble a crescent moon. These people suffer weakness in the kidney, bladder and the corresponding meridians.

The earth hand (fig. 1.10) - This hand is thick, short, wide and chubby. The palm is square-shaped and the fingers are short and thick, with slow-growing squarish nails. Here the weakness is in the spleen, pancreas, stomach, joints and nerve endings. Following with the marches, there are many authors who advocate the theory than Man is a summarised microcosmic version of the Universe, and that his structure reflects the material, astral and divine planes that constitute this microcosm, out thir dimension. They believe that our physical body is just a wrapping on a frame. To them, that "something" or shapin body acts in Man in the same way that the starts act in the Universe, and they call in the "astral body". This hypothesis, which has caught on in recent years, holds that the physical boyd is a result of the astral body, which in turn is directly influenced by the spirit.

Continuing with the number three, each of these bodies matches or is connected to its own area: the material body to the abdominal area, the astral body to the thoracic area, and the divine body to the cephalic. Furthermone, each centre or area is connected to a pair of limbs that demonstrate the influence of this centre within Nature. Our abdomen is connected to our feet and legs, out thorax to our arms and hands and oru head to the cephalic members (maxillar and larynx).

If our hands are connected to the astral realm that is home to the shaping forces, our

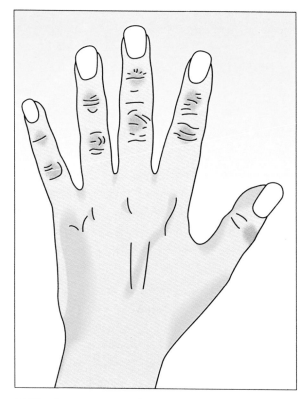

■ *Fig I.9. A water hand is short and spatular, swollen and deep with a blackish hue.*

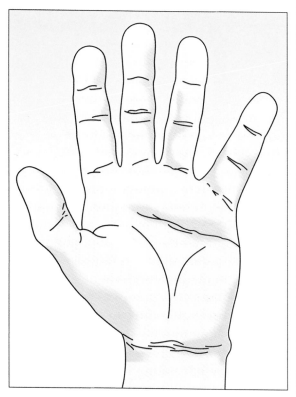

■ *Fig. I.10. An earth hand is thick, short, broad and plump.*

hands are the organ of Man's life centre, which is why twenty-four hous after death the lines of the hands start to fade away, starting with the tinnest ones.

Now we will look at the different parts of the hand, remembering that the hand is a whole and must be interpreted as such, as we have explained above.

CHAPTER II

SHAPES
OF THE HANDS

I n this chapter we are going to look at the shapes, size and general colour of the hands; or, to put it another way, the outer shell or co-tainer, what can be seen at first sight, the parts that we cannot hide and that reflect our personality.

To do so, for one moment let's imagine that our hands are two maps that faithfully reflect the geography of our life, just as maps describe the geography of the Earth. We know that the Earth is subject to attack both on the inside and on the outside, and that these attacks alter and change its geography. Similarly, our hands change shape as a result of the life experiences that change us.

Moreover, aerial maps of the planets (which are obtained from photographs taken by artificial satellites) show that each planet is spherical and of different colours. The Earth is blue, the Moon silvery-white and Mars is reddish. Though each human race is characterized by a different colour, generally speaking our hands may tend to be more reddish, greyish, white or yellowish. The colour of a planet will depend on its atmosphere, its temperature and the minerals and chemical products inside it. Similarly, the colour of our hands will depend on the physical and psychical constitution of each individual.

The stars also vary in size and density, so their properties also vary. In the same way, someone who has large hands will not have the same characteristics as someone who has ordinary or small hands.

The mountains, rivers, valleys, oceans and continents appear on our left-hand map, just as they were formed when we were born. As our lives go by, they all change shape to reflect the effect that life's experiences have on us.

Whereas the map on our left hand changes from day to day, our right-hand map outlines the projects that we want to carry out and the changes that must occur in our life's geography if we are to carry them out.

Translated into the language of chirology,

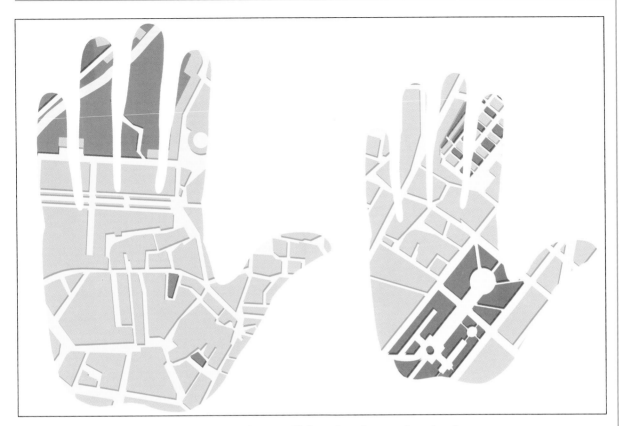

■ *Fig II.1. Our capacity to analyze or synthesize will depend on the size of our hand.*

our left hand maps our present and all our past experiences, while the right hand reflects our projects for the future and their current state. If we use this arrangement in hand reading, we will be much more ready to accept what the Bible says: "Long life is in her right hand, in her left hand are riches and honour" (Proverbs 3:16).

It has already been sufficiently proven that the right hand corresponds to the left hemisphere of the brain (which harbours our creative initiative), and that left hand is related to the right hemisphere, which is our data bank. That is why with a left-handed patient you must find out which is the strongest hand, and then read it as if it was the right hand.

THE SIZE OF THE HANDS

If we had to draw a map to explain or show a place to someone, and we only had a tiny scrap of paper, most likely we would try to list the most interesting details. In our effort to summarize the information and make the most of the piece of paper, in the end the map would be so sketchy and simple that it would hardly be of any use to anyone. We might cause confusion and mislead people by leaving out important details, even though the size of the map would give a fairly good overall view of the area. An added advantage is that we would not take very long to draw it, and the other person would not waste time trying to understand it.

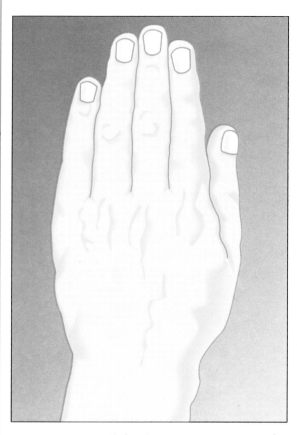

■ *Fig II.2. A wide hand suggests expansion, vitality and happiness. Sometimes its frankness and spontaneity can be thoughtless.*

On the other hand, if we had enough time, we would probably draw the map in great detail. We would correct any mistakes we might have made in the small map, adding in any information we could think of, however insignificant. It would be much closer to reality and much more accurate, but the other person would not find it so easy and quick to use. It would also take us longer to draw, and the map would lack the global view offered by the small map.

The size of someone's hands are the main sign of what they contain and of the person's skills and qualities. Always in the total context of a person's size, people who have small hands can see things from a global viewpoint (fig. II.1), but dislike painstaking tasks and detail. They take in everything that is happening around them, and take fast decisions; but they may mistakes if they rush into things. Small hands are primary and intuitive, and are not fooled by appearances; such people are ruled by their heart rather than their mind, and are swayed by intuition rather than by thought. Since they move and act so fast, they are disorderly, impulsive and fanciful; yet they are capable of accomplishing great feats without taking orders from anyone.

People with large hands tend to analyze everything right down to the last detail. They are just the right people for slow, painstaking jobs in fields such as research, mathematics, surgery, science and watch-making. They take their time when making a decision, because first they thoroughly analyze and examine the pros and cons; yet once they have made their mind up there's no going back and they defend their view staunchly. They are discreet, are good listeners and know how to keep a secret. Sincere and proud, they find it hard to adapt to new situations, and tends to let themselves be dragged along by the impulse of the small-handed people. In large hands the brain rules over the heart.

People with ordinary or medium-sized hands have the advantages and drawbacks of large and small-handed people. They can analyze or summarize to their heart's content, depending on what is happening to them. Although they do not stand out in any particular subject, they manage to overcome anything that is put before them and come out with flying colours thanks to their adaptability. They behave in different ways at different times, taking in even the smallest details without losing sight of the overall vision.

In brief, depending on the size of our hands, our energy will take longer or shorter to cover the space within them; so the bigger the hand, the longer the energy will circulate, thus taking much more notice of details; in the smaller hands there will only be time for an overall glimpse.

Hands are also wide or narrow. Width suggests expansion and narrowness suggests reserve, which is why wide-handed people (fig. II.2) are individuals who long to externalize and pour out their thoughts and wants, confiding them to other people. They are generous and share everything, convinced that those who give, will get. They love challenges, are strong, determined and lively, and normally attract others by seducing them with their joy; they yearn for success and a prosperous life, yet not to the extent of hoarding. They spend money as soon as they earn it. They are trusting and optimistic, pass their happiness onto others and urge their peers to follow suit, blinded by their strength and courage. Yet they can be overly frank and thoughtless, speaking their mind at any point without any measure of diplomacy, so they can seem rude and insensitive. They hurt other people unwittingly because they never keep what they think to themselves, even if nobody has asked them for their opinion.

In contrast, narrow-handed people are proud, weak and distrusting (fig. II.3). They find it hard to adapt and shy away from making commitments. They are not sincere when asked to give an opinion, and usually try to disguise or hide their real thoughts. Even so, they are very good at keeping secrets, and their discretion makes them essential in any association or job that calls for professional secrecy. Yet they have a difficult, taciturn character and may seem misfits.

Hands are either of a soft or a hard consis-tency. A hard hand is a sign of strength and physical activity, a high level of responsibility and a very good state of health. Soft-handed people love to feel surrounded by comfort and well-being. They will get whatever they want, because they are imaginative and are lovers of independence. A soft hand is the hand of an intellectual, a writer or poet, of anyone and everyone who loves intellectual toils and shuns physical effort. If a hand is so soft that it seems flabby, its owner has very little willpower, lacks energy and finds it hard to keep at the same activity for a long time. They may over-do it in the pleasures of life (food, alcohol or sex) to such an extent they often let themselves be swept away.

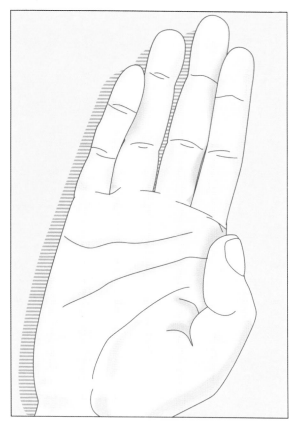

■ *Fig II.3. A narrow hand causes introversion and gives concentration.*

FLEXIBILITY

If we compare our hands to a tree, with our wrist representing the roots, our palm the trunk and our fingers the branches, what we will be looking at is firmly-planted hands that unyieldingly stand up to the air and the elements of Nature. Others, on the contrary, are extremely flexible, and yield at the slightest pressure.

Just how flexible our hands are is a sign of our capacity to have a flexible mind; so people with flexible hands readily accept new ideas, though they find it hard to concentrate and cannot do one thing at a time. They are unpredictable in their acts and feelings, very impressionable and take orders easily. They are so generous that others may take advantage of them, especially so if they also have a very flexible thumb.

A hard-handed person is cautious, responsible and works hard but is stubborn and takes badly to new situations and new ideas. He likes secrets and does not share his feelings or his problems.

COLOUR

First and foremost, it is the colour of a hand that reveals the depth of our patient's soul. Whatever we are interpreting in a hand will mean one thing or another, depending on the colour that goes with it. Importance lies not only in the overall colour of a hand: any line, mountain, phalanx, finger, and even any detail, however small, will be accompanied by a different hue. At first glance, our skin seems to be of a single colour, but if we take the time to observe it thoroughly enough, we will notice stronger colours, duller colours, and the whole spectrum of reds, yellows, browns and blues.

The same happens if you look at a picture of someone who is wearing a white dress. If you look at it from a prudent distance, the artist makes you think that the dress is white, but if you move closer to the picture you will see that each brushstroke of the clothes is a different hue of grey; though overall the brushstrokes convey the sensation of a uniform white colour.

Colour is the impression that rays of light produce on the retina of our eye after being reflected by an object. Ignoring the fact that we still do not know the exact nature of light, we could define it as a form of energy that lights up objects and makes them visible; if we apply this definition to hand-reading, it shows us that colours, as parts of light, clarify and illuminate the messages already offered by the lines on our hand. Colour plays such an important and deeply-rooted role in our culture that now tests are being performed to see if it can be used to cure illnesses, with highly positive results. This technique goes by the name of chromotherapy.

Even so, each colour causes a different sensation in us; some provoke passion and desire while others calm us. By analyzing these faculties when they appear in our hands, we will understand their meanings.

Generally speaking, white, red and yellow are the colours that stand out most in our skin.

White

In the West, white means pureness and chastity and is used in the liturgy of births and weddings. In India it symbolizes the absence of malice and is related to innocence. And even though in the East there was a time when it was identified with mourning, whenever it is used in religious ceremonies it symbolizes cleanliness and purity. For alchemists it represents opening up to the light, and if one bears in mind that light is white, this is its best definition.

White is the beginning and the end, the birth and death of the different transmutations, and it signifies the absolute. A white hand is a sign of inner peace and calm, although such people prefer a life of luxury and pleasure to hard work and toil. They tend to be dominated by material desires and have great sex appeal. However, white spots or areas in any type of coloured hand are very good signs. Depending on where they appear, they will mean happiness, a large amount of money or that we are about to achieve something we wanted and were waiting for - especially if it is a very bright white.

Red

Red is a warm colour. It symbolizes passion, feelings, anger, arousal, desire and pent-up desire struggling to flow and manifest themselves. It is the colour of blood, which is why it is related to life and also to death and destruction.

Whenever we have made an effort, or feel slightly embarrassed, blood rushes to our face and lights it up, making us blush. Some people believe that this colour gives energy, vitality, and heats and improves our blood circulation. It also stimulates adrenalin, the production of red blood cells, periods and sexual power. It also reinforces courage and willpower.

Reddish hands are active, expansive and temperamental. Such people will have passionate qualities and defects, be physical and cerebrally energetic; impatient, full of fighting spirit, ambitious and irritable. Someone who has bright-red hands may be very long-suffering, putting up with harsh situations without complaining or fighting back.

Red areas that stand out against the general colour of the hand denote trials, irritating or unpleasant moments, and may even warn of a possible illness. Any line, sign or mount that is coloured red denotes problems in that area. If the red darkens or turns purplish, it is a symptom that the problem is reaching worrying proportions.

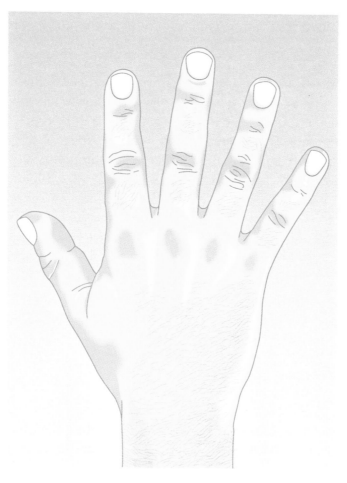

■*Fig II.4. Too much hair on the back of a hand indicates a liking for the material things in life.*

25

Yellow

Yellow hands denote a bilious temperament, and it is the colour of people whose mind always rule their heart. First they calculate, then they act, so they seem astute and intelligent, even if they are not. Their reason always holds their intuition in check. They tend to be excessively strict or fanatical.

Yellow is said to inspire and rouse the mind, strengthening the nerves, helping reason and self-control, improving the state of the skin, and it is supposed to be the best brain and nerve stimulant.

When it appears somewhere in the hand, and stands out against the general colour, it may be a sign of liver and digestive problems, or also nervous fatigue. At psychic level it can indicate events that provoke negative feelings of hate or envy.

THE HAIR

Very hairy hands denote a love of the material things in life and a great intelligence. Man and woman alike, our whole body is covered in hair, except for the soles of our feet and palms of our hands, though sometimes it is only a very fine layer that is barely visible. So when we talk about hair, we refer to the hair on the back of someone's hand (fig. II.4).

Someone who has no hair at all on his hands may be lacking in vitality and virility, and have an unstable character and effeminate feelings, especially if that person is a man. Yet we will get a better idea of what hair means if we combine it with the colour of the hands. Broadly speaking, people with hairy red hands tend to be jealous (fig. II.5), hairy yellow hands show a very intelligent person and hairy white hands have an excessive sexuality.

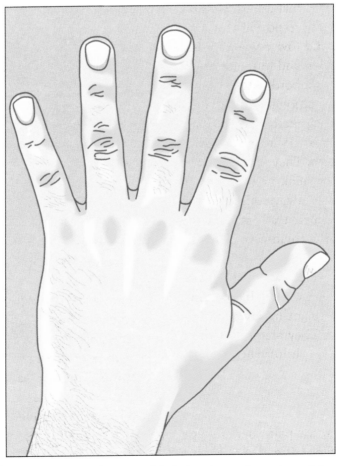

■ *Fig II.5. A hairy, reddish hand may be a sign of jealousy.*

THE SHAPES

Hands are a wide range of shapes, despite being very like each other; our right hand may be slightly different from our left hand. Experience has shown that shapes can vary a lot from one person to another, and even from one hand to another. Therefore the best course of action is to simplify their meanings, dividing them into three general categories so that we can give a broad definition of everyone's characteristic tendencies. Any other shapes that we come across will just be combinations of these three. We will refer to them as the "square hand", "spatular hand" and "cone-shaped hand".

Square hand

In a square hand, the palm forms a square or rectangle (fig. II.6). In other words, the distance from the base of the thumb to the other side of the hand equals the distance between the base of the fingers and the joint with the hand.

Square-handed people are methodical, tidy and practical. They love organizing, so they are well-equipped for jobs that call for method and calculation. They are responsible, with a noble sense of justice and love law and order, but are slaves to tradition and form. They try to look intelligently for subordinates who use their instinct and imagination in order to help them; although with their method, objectivity and positivism they will try to watch over, advise and organize them. They are good planners, and just as good at making others carry them out. Yet they are always fair and just and take the blame if their team fails; sincerity is a norm both for themselves and for others.

They need regular rest, which they use calmly to order their ideas. They like a calm, peaceful family life, implanting laws and traditions in their home. They are at their best talking about politics or philosophy.

Spatular hand

As its name indicates, the palm of this type of hand is spatula-shaped (fig. II.7). In this case, the hand is narrower at the bottom (i.e., the wrist, or from the base of the thumb to

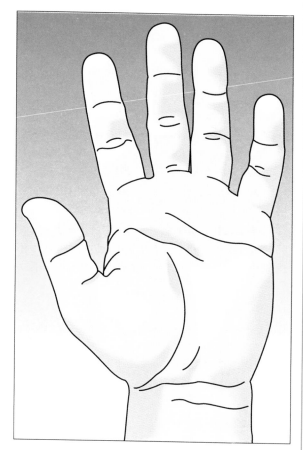

■ *Fig II.6. Square hand, also known as the orthodox hand.*

the opposite side of the hand) than the distance across the hand at the base of the fingers.

People who have this type of hand are full of energy and intuition. They work tirelessly to the point of nervous exhaustion, always have to be on the move, and love fighting and battling. This can lead them to the brink of illness because they fail to realize just how much energy they are losing.

They are ideal workers for carrying out the plans established by square-handed people, but in terms of character they are independent, not too thoughtful and lack any method.

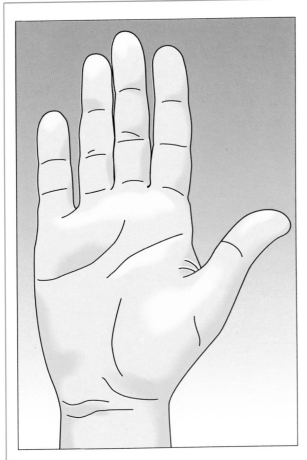

Spatular-handed people execute square-handed peoples' orders boldly and with conviction. They are stopped only by illness, once they have used up their reserves of energy. They are very fond of all types of animals, which they look after and protect, and their sense of fidelity makes them great lovers.

The cone-shaped hand

In a cone-shaped hand, the distance from the thumb to the opposite edge of the hand is longer than the side-to-side distance at the base of the fingers (fig. II.8).

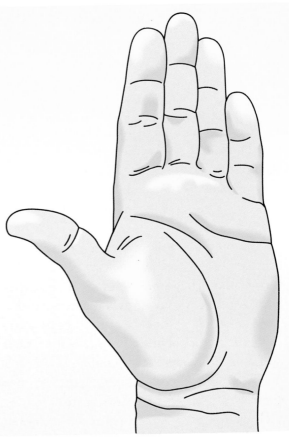

■ *Fig II.8. Cone-shaped hand, the hand of reason and intuition.*

Moreover, they are none too fond of having other people watch or organize them. Their courage and bravery leads them to perform great works for the good of mankind or any job that involves a challenge.

As soon as they have completed their mission fast and easily, they immediately set out to look for another. Their enormous self-confidence may make them seem self-centred and conceited, yet you will not find as loyal a friend, and their superiors will commend them tasks in the knowledge that no-one can do a better job, although they will not let anyone else interfere, or manipulate them.

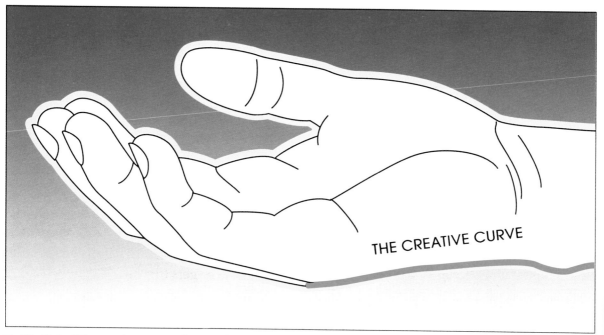

THE CREATIVE CURVE

■ *Fig II.9. The creative curve or karate chop.*

This is the hand of reason and intuition. These people are energetic and hard-working, may be realists or dreamers, lovers of beauty and highly independent. Their great imagination tends to steer them towards the humanities, plastic arts, painting, architecture, poetry or sculpture.

Yet they analyze and check everything because they always have their feet firmly on the ground. They sometimes act like square-handed people or, if and when necessary, like spatular-handed people; so whenever they criticize the actions of other types of people, their opinions are always well-founded.

As we pointed out at the start, we may come across hands with contradictory shapes, such as a square-shaped palm with cone or spatula-shaped fingers, or a spatula-shaped palm with cone or square-shaped fingers. If we apply our definitions of the meaning of the shapes and what the palm or fingers represent, we will find our client's virtues and defects.

The creative curve or karate chop

This external shape that is drawn on our hands, from the wrist to the base of the small finger, is a very useful aid in discovering a person's creative capacity (fig. II.9). It is also called the "karate chop" (because it is the part of the hand used in that noble sport for hitting.)

We should remember that this edge of the hand is the border of the Mount of Mercury (our intellectual intelligence), of the Mount of Mars (our capacity to act) and of the Mount of the Moon (our imaginative intelligence).

This edge is also the source of the Heart

Line and the end of the Head Line. If we blend strength, intellect, imagination and feelings, we will bring together the best weapons for obtaining wisdom. However, to find out which weapon everyone handles best, we must see which part of the curve is widest (fig. II.10).

If your curve is widest at the Mount of Mercury, you are intellectually creative, have great force of character and the capacity to overcome any intellectual or spiritual misfortune. You are psychically strong but physically weak.

If the widest part of the curve is the Mount of the Moon, you are physically strong and get your energy from your body. You shrug off illness and are very un-

likely to suffer serious complaints, because even if you do fall ill, you get better in no time at all. Yet psychically you are highly vulnerable, especially if there is a long or deep cleft at the start of your Heart Line.

If the widest part is near Mars, and the whole edge of the hand forms a lovely half-moon, you are physically and psychically well-balanced, and have energy and creativity in both realms.

In any of these three cases, if the apex is more marked on your left hand than on your right, it means that you are not making the best use of the strength and energy that you inherited when you were born. If the opposite is true, you have increased your talents with your own willpower.

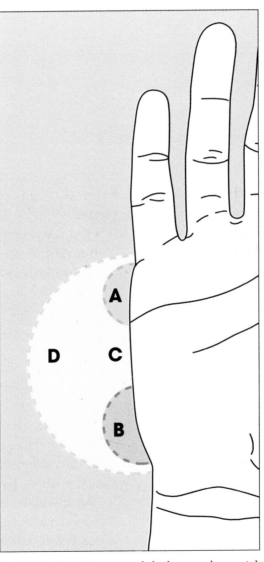

■ *Fig II.10. Diagram of the karate chop, with the different widths. A) In Mercury; B) In the Moon; C) In Mars. D) The curve of creativity.*

CHAPTER III

THE SKIN

Our skin, which is the organ that covers and protects our whole body, and at the same time displays our external image, not only gives us accurate information about our environment but also all the information about our interior. For centuries, we have allowed doctors to diagnose us by examining the colour, temperature and consistency of our skin. Yet we are still reluctant to admit that the skin is a source of information on our state of mind; we find it hard to believe that the mind uses our skin to sketch each and every one of the experiences that we live, and to outline any plans that we may have for the future.

The fact of the matter is that our skin does indeed resemble an artist's canvas on which our brain, helped by our nerve endings, accurately depicts each of the passages of our life, scene by scene. It also draws outlines of the scenes that we may act out in the future, and which we will complete later on, giving them the texture and colour necessary to complete the painting (fig. III.1).

Of course, when we record our life's events on our skin we do not paint them in a traditional, academic way. On the contrary, we can use light and shade, relief, different colour changes, glazes, or draw perfect lines or symbols that in themselves discover countless meanings. Each of us is like a group of master painters who contribute with their different techniques towards the construction of a single work: our own.

This is the human being's reality, and any one who has the right skills can see it. Therefore a chirologist's task is only to interpret this reality, without having to make use of other paranormal abilities such as clear-sightedness. A chirologist's source of information is always his patient's skin, and in his patient's hands, feet and face he will find an excellent resumé of the whole body.

Looking for drawings on the skin of someone's hands can be as exciting as watching an

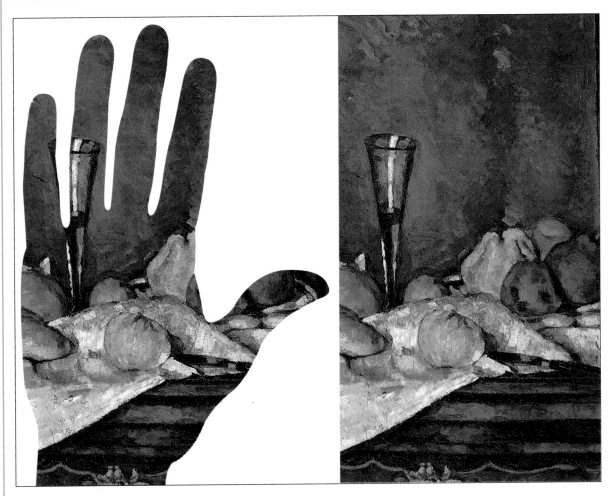

■ *Fig. III.1. Our skin reflects all the events that affect our mind.*

action-packed film. The difference is that our hands reflect real events that have happened, are happening or will happen. However, professional chirologists fail to agree on this perfectly demonstrable reality, and have formed two streams of thought: some use only the lines to interpret, while others make their interpretations by comparing the skin with the celluloid of a film, which records all the images that have passed through our mind.

In my early days as a palmist, one event showed me that even memories that we have

erased from our mind are reflected in our hands and can, once discovered, help us to cure phobias and habits of an unknown origin.

When I was talking to a patient about painting, she remarked to me that for many years she had been suffering from a phobia for which she could find no explanation. As a result of her phobia, she found it impossible to go into a museum, church or even a relative's home if there was a portrait hanging on the wall. If, due to a commitment, she ever had to enter such a place, after a while she would start to feel dizzy and sometimes even fainted if she was foolish enough to stay in the room any longer. However, if the motif of the painting was a still-life or landscape, she had no problem and could stay there a long time without feeling any of the aforementioned symptoms.

That conversation aroused my curiosity, so I asked her to let me see her hands, to try to see if my theories pointed in the right direction and that our entire subconscious is reflected on our hands. When I looked at her left hand, what I saw just below the start of the birth line (which represents the first years of our lives) was a picture of a man pushing a woman against a wall and attacking her with a knife (fig. II.2). When I described the bloody scene to her, she recalled that when she

was a child, at her grandparents' house she always used to sleep in a bedroom where there was a portrait of a great-aunt. As well as having the same name as her, her great-aunt looked extraordinarily like her.

Then she told me that her great-uncle had murdered her great-aunt in a fit of jealousy, many years before my patient had been born; and even though she could not have witnessed the scene, her grandparents had described it to her so vividly that her imagination had recorded it as if she had been there. So at last my patient had found the root of her fears and was able to confront and solve her problem.

This case fully convinced me that our unconscious uses our skin to warn us of anything that may be harming us, even if we are not conscious of it. Delving deeper into the subject, I gradually found that, as well as being reflected on the skin in different ways (fig. III.3), certain types of warnings issue specific alarm signals that continue if we do not heed them and that only disappear when the matter in question has passed or been dealt with. These alarm signals take the form of red spots -that stand out against the hand's normal colour- blisters, pimples, warts, blackheads, moles, peeling, chilblains, callouses, cuts, burns and wounds.

Generally speaking, if the problem is solved fully and we draw the right conclusions from it, the alarm signal will disappear as fast as it appeared; but if we do not solve it, the signals will persist and we will feel discomfort and worry. Who doesn't remember, at some stage, having been worried when a red spot appeared on their hand?

Once again, a case that I examined showed me the meaning of these red spots.

A patient told me that a red spot had come out on her right hand, on the fleshy elevation

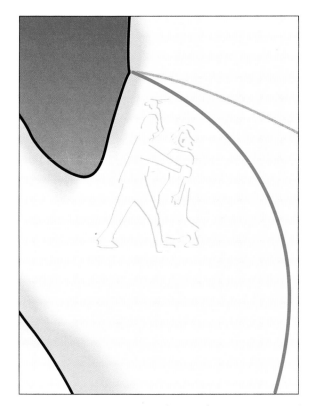

■ *Fig. III.2. Even scenes that we have not witnessed may appear on our hands.*

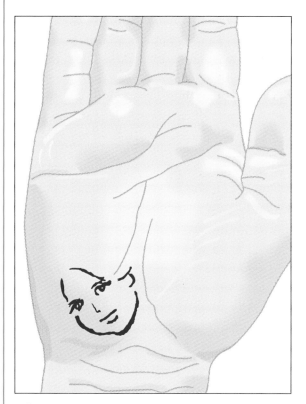

■ *Fig. III.3. The faces of people who impress us or play an important role in our lives are reflected on our skin.*

that we all have below the base of the thumb. When I looked at her hand I saw that there was a square around the spot and that, inside it, other smaller lines forming drawings that looked to me like a wardrobe, beds and two bedside tables. The layout of the furniture reminded my patient of her and her husband's bedroom (fig. III.4). Since the red spot was above the bed, I imagined that the warning had to do with problems in their relationship; but the position –the Mount of Venus– meant that the problem was also related to children, family and pleasures. Finally she confided to me that she had just had her third child, and did not want to have any more. In fact, she was obsessed with the idea of becoming pregnant. Out of respect for her intimacy, I did

not ask how she solved the problem, but the fact is that the red spot had disappeared a few weeks later and she did not have any more children.

Blisters - These tend to be caused by an external irritation that causes an eruption of fluids on the skin (fig. III.5). On the basis of what we said in the previous chapter, we can interpret blisters as being caused by mental and emotional disorders that come out onto the surface through a weak spot of the skin, caused by an external event that irritates us. Later on we will look at the different parts of the hand, so we will be able to know which weak spot is attacking us.

Pimples and warts - Pimples and warts are more persistent and take much longer to heal or disappear, so they are a sign that the exter-

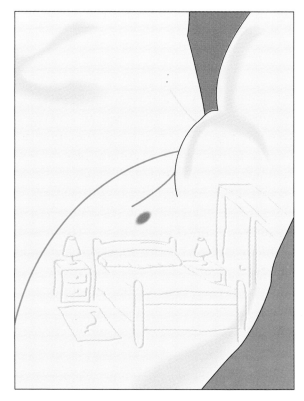

■ *Fig. III.4. Red spots are a warning from our sub-conscious.*

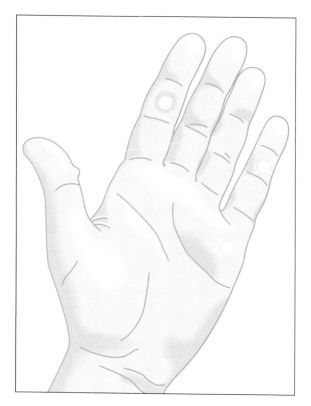

■ *Fig. III.5. Blisters or surface irritation that conceal internal irritation.*

birth, others emerge at different points of our lives; and as if by whim, sometimes they seem blacker while at other times they become duller or their colour fades. The fact of the matter is that these small dark-pigmented spots, which seem to appear on our skin by chance, are signs that mark hidden capacities that remain latent within us, waiting for us to decide to make use of them.

They are rather like small objects of value that we brought with us when we were born into this world, after leaving that other world to which we may have belonged before our material body took shape. If moles appear on the back of our hands, it is a sign that the hidden skills have not shown themselves yet. However, if they appear on the palm of our hand it means that, albeit unconsciously, at certain points of our lives we use a special

nal irritation has been more intense (fig. III.6). The external event is more painful; it forces us to revise negative concepts that lie inside us. We are torn between accepting the experience or clinging onto mistaken thoughts of the past. It is a annoying, persistent situation, and if we fail to deal with it honestly it could well become embedded within us.

Moles - Moles are so important that they deserve special attention, to such an extent that many students of the occult sciences regard them as having a divinatory power, and a very close-knit relationship with the inner nature of the person in question. This fortune-telling practice goes by the name of Melanomancy and consists of interpreting the moles that appear anywhere on the body. Although some moles may appear on us at

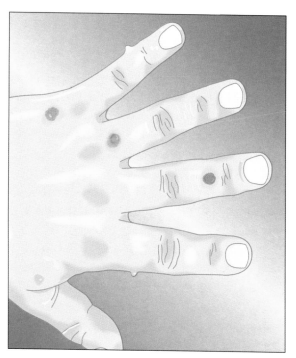

■ *Fig. III.6. Spots and warts or irritating thoughts of the past that have flourished again.*

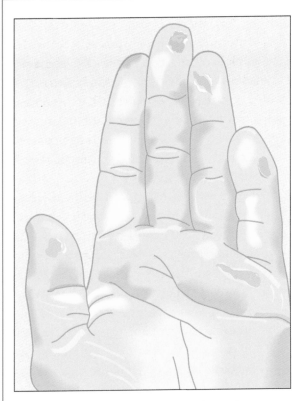

■ *Fig. III.7. Peeling. A change of skin indicates inner changes.*

intuition to solve problems that are related to the area of our hand where the mole appears.

If a mole becomes dull or its colours fades, it is warning us that we may be overusing its powers. If we rest from the activity that is forcing us to use its powers, the mole will become replenished with colour and energy.

Peeling - When our skin starts to peel, it transforms itself; it sheds the dry, dead cell to make way for a younger, finer and smoother skin (fig. III.7) If we translate this circumstance into our own particular language, it means that we are discarding old patterns and starting to consider other, more up-to-date forms of thought that are more to our advantage. In a word, we are accepting positive changes in our life.

Chilblains - Chilblains are caused by poor blood circulation and usually appear when it is very cold (fig. III.8). They are a sign of emotional coldness, perhaps because we are afraid of facing up to or committing ourselves to other people, which involves pouring out the emotional energy that lies within us. This attitude may be causing us mental pain and sore, hurt feelings, the same physical symptoms as produced by the chilblains.

Callouses - We have already explained the meaning of callouses in the introduction, but since they are so frequent and easy to locate we shall talk about them in greater detail.

We said that a callous is the sign of a mental conflict that arises when our mind is too weak and frightened to deal with a certain aspect of our life. It is a shield that protects us, but it may make us insensitive or indiffe-

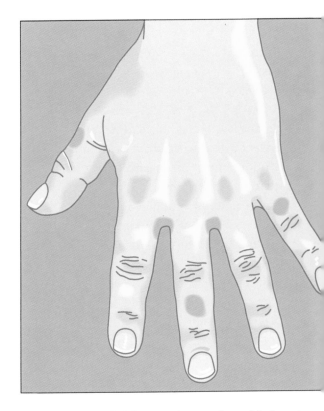

■ *Fig. III.8. Chilblains indicate a fear of facing up to our feelings.*

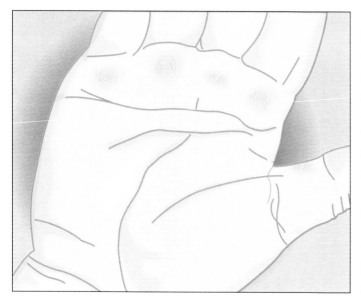

■ *Fig. III.9. Callouses or hard skin indicate weaknesses.*

rent towards other people. It indicates an inverted movement of energy; we do not let it flow freely, we concentrate it at one point so much that it turns into hardened or corneous tissue.

A callous that is a thin layer of skin will have formed only a short while ago, so the conflict will also be recent; but a thick layer of hardened skin will have roots that reach the flesh under the skin, meaning that it arose a long time ago. Therefore it indicates a long-standing mental problem (fig. III.9).

Nonetheless, I would like to make it quite clear that I am neither judging nor reject calloused hands; quite the contrary: I am convinced that our mind quite wisely protects and looks after our body, and also looks after itself with the self-denial typical of a devoted mother; and when it puts up protective barriers, it is because we need them in order to progress well in life. Of course, if a callous hurts or becomes especially annoying, we will have to reconsider our attitude and our thoughts.

Cuts, burns, wounds - (fig. III.10) - Interpreting these signs is a difficult task because we might go into the psychology of the accident and be forced to ask ourselves whether it has been the result of a fatal stroke of bad luck or, on the contrary, whether we ourselves are attracting it with our attitude and our negative thoughts.

By way of example I will describe an incident in which I cut myself.

A few years ago I had to give a lift to somebody with whom I had to do business. I am not very careful with my car and normally don't keep it too tidy, so I was worried that the gentleman might get a mistaken impression of me.

To make things worse, when he got into my car he knocked the rear-view mirror, which fell onto the floor. In my haste to put it back in its place, while my passenger and I were apologizing to each other I cut the tip of the index finger of my right hand, though not very seriously.

When I was looking at the cut later on, I realized that I had cut a finger which, in terms of chirology, is related to the individual's personality. At the time my sole concern had been to tidy up my untidy car and so impress my passenger. As a result, my brain was unable to operate its defense mechanisms and make me withdraw my finger before I cut it.

We have a mental capacity to anticipate events that have not happened yet, so injuries —especially injuries to the back of our hands— warn us of events that will bother us in the near future. Normally we hurt ourselves just when the event is happening, even though we may not realize at that moment.

Sometimes the injury or wound is so deep that it leaves a scar to remind us permanently

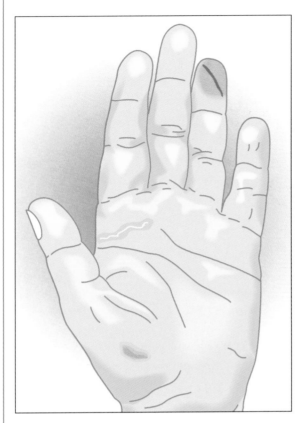

■ *Fig. III.10. Injuries or a lack of attention of our unconscious defence mechanism.*

that we must deal with the problem as best as we can.

If we manage to interpret these signals correctly, not only do they help us to become better acquainted with ourselves, but they also foster and develop communication with our own unconscious, as long as we do not turn it into a slave-driving habit.

In short, the general texture of our skin affords basic information about our personality and our behaviour. The smoother and finer our skin, the more vulnerable we will be to our environment at a physical level; yet psychically we will be braver and stronger, and will not need shields or armour to protect ourselves. Therefore our feelings will be more fluent and we will express them better.

On the other hand, the drier, harsher, harder and flaky our skin is, the less our health will be affected by external factors such as temperature or pollution; but illnesses will emerge as a result of our own repressed feelings until they overwhelm us or make us ill. We know that our mind is weak, or at least has weak parts, because our hardened skin is a sign that we are hiding certain fears beneath a mask of toughness.

If after reading all this you still want to probe the landscapes, faces, buildings, people and animals that are sketched on your skin, all you need is a little patience, a little concentration and a good deal of interest. They will help you discover your entire inner world, portrayed in images.

CHAPTER IV

THE MOUNTS OR FLESHY PADS

According to Greek mythology, at the dawn of time Heaven wed the Earth and together they had many children, the most famous of whom were Cybele and Themis, the first goddesses, and Titan, Saturn and Hephaestus, the first-born gods.

When Heaven saw how skilled and bold his offspring were, he was filled with envy and threw them into the Underworld. Yet Earth became enraged at the lot of her children, so she freed them and helped them to fight their father. Saturn conquered Heaven and took over the world throne.

All the adventures and stories about the heroes and demi-gods of mythology start in this way, and such stories form the foundations of subsequent religions, as well as the very psychological essence of Man.

Let's imagine that we are the descendants of this race of gods, and that we have inherited virtues and defects from them. If we use the palms of our hands to locate the energy we have inherited from our first fathers, the gods, we could divide our palms into sections, into cells, domains or abodes, where each god would have his kingdom. However, we must never forget that each palm is like a small Olympus where all the gods work together as a team, without forgoing their own, personal traits.

In chirology these abodes are known as Mounts or Fleshy Pads. They are located at the base of each finger and are related to the type of energy that is channelled towards that part of the hand. They represent aspects of our character that are symbolized by mythological beings (fig. IV.1).

As is to be expected, each of us will have inherited more qualities from one god than from another, so our mounts or abodes will not always be the same. Moreover, similarities or likings may have made us look after certain qualities more than others, so our mounts will not be as they were at birth, nor will they be the same on one hand as on the other. If we want to find out which qualities are most important in our character, we only have to feel the fleshy pads or the depressions and

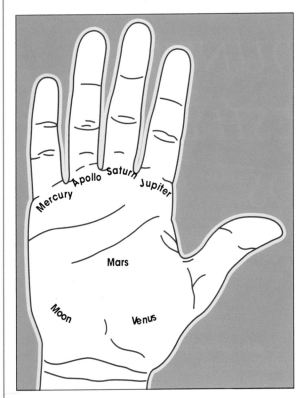

■ *Fig. IV.1. The mounts or fleshy pads of the hands, with the name of their respective mythological gods.*

plains of our palms; in doing so we will note if they are low, high or normal; if they are hard or soft; or if some overlap others.

If one mount blends into another, it means a blend of qualities, as if the gods who rule the mounts had decided to join forces to make it faster to use them.

If the mount is hard, it means that we are using that god's qualities energetically. If it is soft, we are not using that mount's qualities enough. A high mount means an abundance of qualities, and if it is low we hardly make any use of the god's qualities.

When you are studying the mounts, remember that not only do they represent traits of our character: they also indicate personalized areas of the hand where we record our life experiences. This pattern of organiza-

tion will allow us to discover a specific fact if we know what has caused it. We simply have to look for it in the right place.

SATURN

Saturn is the symbol of time, which is why he devoured his children, who represented the years that he himself created. He was the first god to decree laws, and he also laid down rules to achieve peace between Heaven and Earth. Yet he can be ruthless and cruel, because he is a constant reminder that we are subject to life and death.

According to the Cabbala, he is regarded as the Great Architect of the Inner Temple that we can all build inside ourselves, if we keep to his rules. Consequently, his mount is at the base of the middle finger, or Saturn's finger (fig. IV.2). The Mount of Saturn contains the most important tendon of the hand, and is the point of origin of the other fingers' tendons. Moreover, as we will see further on, the two main lines of our hand, the fate line and the heart line, usually end at this mount.

The Mount of Saturn lets us balance our reason and ideals with a view to our own self-development; it reveals the inward-looking aspect of our personality. In short, it is the balancing force of human personality.

An ordinary mount represents responsibility, self-preservation, the internal quest for truth, love of independence and solitude. A mount that is too high may prompt fears, superstitions, sadness, melancholy, or too much analysis and rigidness.

This mount will show us how likely we are to suffer fractures or accidents, how much time we have left to solve a certain problem satisfactorily and whether we believe in good or bad luck. It also reveals our social, political or religious ideas and our occult skills.

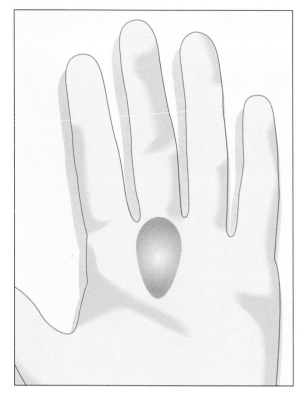

■ *Fig. IV.2. Mount of Saturn at the base of the middle finger.*

JUPITER

Jupiter is a domineering god who rules with a fist of iron, although he shares out his kingdom. He is just and fair, but when angered his vengeance knows no bounds. Even so, he was the first god to place his trust in Man, and though once he decided to exterminate Mankind, he spared one couple, leaving them to repopulate the Earth. Often he does not mind taking on a human form, and even goes so far as falling in love with mortal women. He is autodidactic, gives the mortals moral rules and forces them to abide by them, showing them the advantages of being human and punishing anyone who tries to go up to Heaven, such as the Giants.

Jupiter represents the expansion of the individual, whatever we display to the outer world, as compared to the inward-looking aspect of our personality that is represented by Saturn. Jupiter is home to ambition, pride, vanity and self-centredness, together with the tendency to domineer.

The Mount of Jupiter is at the base of the index finger (fig. IV.3), also known as the finger of Jupiter, and this mount is connected to the three main lines of the hand, because the life line and mental line start below it, and the heart line normally ends at it. Therefore it is of capital importance.

At the same time, the Mount of Jupiter is home to the father, the husband, the boss and anyone who holds authority or power over us, or anyone else who at least confronts us or competes with our personality. It represents

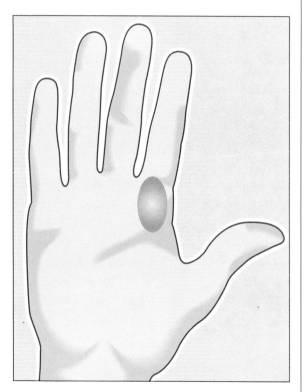

■ *Fig. IV.3. Mount of Jupiter at the base of the index finger.*

justice, a positive outlook on life, idealism, the desire to help others and self-affirmation. However, a flat or very shallow Mount of Jupiter is typical of people who have a very poor opinion of themselves, lack any ambition and the initiative to triumph. They look upon themselves as social misfits and fail to make the most of opportunities.

According to the Cabbala, Jupiter is the promoter of desires, emotions and feelings. He steadily takes over our lives from the moment we are born, issuing orders to the rest of the gods, who must heed and channel such orders through their own personalities.

This the part of the hand will reveal any legal problems, such as court cases, fines or the signing of contracts, of whatever type. it will also show us if we enjoy our job or whether, on the contrary, we find it boring and stifling.

MARS

The Cabbala states that Mars acts in the dark world of our emotions, and shakes them in order to arouse our conscience. Wherever Mars is to be seen there will be passion, feeling and movement that may lead to war. Mars makes things move forward, and forces Man to face the consequences of his acts.

The positive side of Mars fosters our desire to survive, progress and overcome hardships, but the negative side may arouse feelings of hate and revenge within us. The good and bad side of Mars alike may unlock the doors to hate, so both for own sake and for the sake of mankind it is essential that we learn to control this force-desire and channel it positively.

Mars is represented on our hand by two mounts and a plain of the same name, which occupy a strip in the middle of our hand; it separates the four gods, which are the origin of four of the five fingers, from the two goddesses that are located next to the wrist (fig. IV.4).

The plain of Mars is the depression in the middle of our palm. It is the battle field on which all our inner strifes take place. It resembles a Roman amphitheatre where gladiators fought for their lives, and our strifes are watched by the gods in their mounts or abodes, which form a circle around the plain. All the main lines of our hand pass through the plain of Mars, which is where we will discover our personality and emotions. If you press the centre of this plain with your thumb and place your other fingers on the other side of the hand, you will see whether the wall of tissue

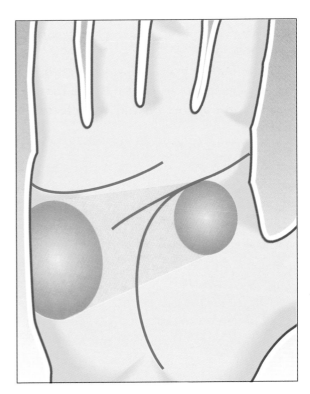

■ *Fig. IV.4. Diagram of the Mounts of Mars. The passive mount is below the Mount of Jupiter. The active mount is in the middle of the creative line.*

is weak or strong. A strong wall is a sign of self-confidence, whereas a weak wall indicates a weak character, someone who is subject to all types of influences. This trait is particularly dangerous in young people.

You can use the same pressure to find the real temperature of the hand and the person's state of nerves. This area of the hand also reveals our working life, skills, chances or hobbies.

Our energy flows from the wrist through the valley of Neptune to this plain, where it is distributed to all the Mounts. Once it has absorbed the personal attitude of each god, it leaves us through the fingers. Energy can also use the same route to reach our interior whenever it needs to.

As we have already pointed out, the two Mounts of Mars are on each side of the plain, because Mars not only fights the other gods, he also fights us, inside us. In short, war is his element.

Therefore the first mount, which is below Jupiter and above Venus, represents the courage and strength we need to fight off attacks and other people's attempts to manipulate us. This mount indicates whether we have been hurt or injured, feel mistreated, give up easily, or whether our pent-up emotions are about to burst out. If so, the mount will be very red and swollen. It is the terrain of our inner struggles, so any defeats or setbacks are dangerous as well as painful because they may lead to traumas, phobias, hate and a lust for revenge, in particular, because it shelters and nourishes the beginning of the head and life lines. Its protective shields are justice and pride, which it receives from Jupiter, and pleasures and beauty, which come from Venus.

The second Mount of Mars is below Mercury and above the Moon; it represents Mars amid the din of battle. It is our daily fight with life, our struggles to get the upper hand. It is home to our capacity to be aggressive. When we confront someone or something, we do so with passion and feeling, often forgetting to use our reason. On our hand this is shown by the fact that the heart line keeps Mars at a safe distance from the cunning and reasonable Mercury, and when the two gods

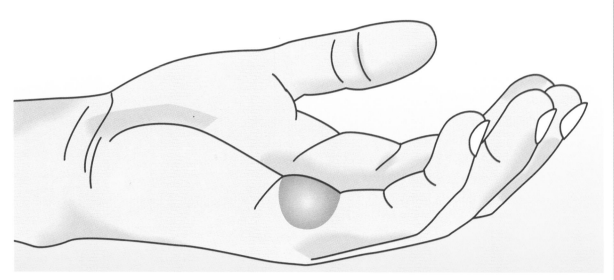

■ *Fig. IV.5. Mount of Mercury at the base of the little finger.*

fail to reach an agreement it acts as an insurmountable barrier. However, our head line usually ends at this mount, or at least goes round it. This eases the conflict a little and means that Mars does not have to fight alone. It is also connected to the Mount of the Moon, which offers Mars its ideas, intuition and fantasies to help him achieve his goals.

The first mount of Mars provides protective shields, but this mount gives us cunning and reason, the weapons we need to attack and which we can take from Mercury, and the intuition offered by the Moon.

Physically, it is the strongest area of the hand and is used in martial arts such as karate.

MERCURY

Tradition has it that Mercury, otherwise known as Hermes by the Greeks, Hemoc by the Hebrews and Thoth by the Egyptians, bequeathed all his hermetic knowledge to Man, and that this gave rise to the whole spectrum of occult sciences.

Mercury is believed to have recorded his wisdom in pictures, nowadays seen in the Tarot or book of Thoth, also known as the book of life, and which contains 108 tables that symbolically record this knowledge for all the initiates who are capable of interpreting them.

It is our most polyvalent mount, it gives us the skill for business, writing, diplomacy and oratory; it helps us to learn languages, teaches us to use sophisms, discover inventions and see how our sexuality works (fig. IV.5). If we also have a long little finger, our abilities will be that much greater. However, if the mount does not look too good and has lots of crossed lines, it may be a sign of a tendency to theft, deceit, evil sexual inclinations, and even criminal impulses, especially if the little finger is curved.

If your mount is very flat, it could mean that you find it hard to communicate with others, especially in a love relationship, because this mount is the point of origin of the heart line, and the relationship and children lines cross it.

APOLLO

The Mount of Apollo is located below the ring finger, between the Mounts of Saturn and Mercury (fig. IV.6). Apollo and Mercury were

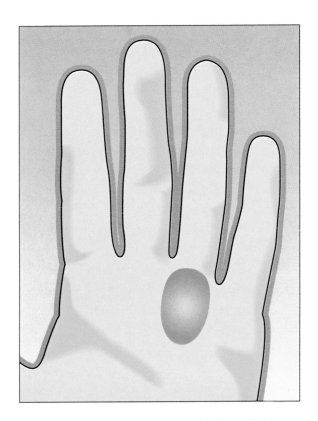

■ *Fig. IV.6. Mount of Apollo at the base of the ring finger.*

always very united and shared common hobbies such as music. They are usually so close to each other on our hands that it is easy to confuse them.

Our character needs this blend because Mercury is practical, scientific, resourceful and commercially-minded, while Apollo provides the pure ideals that balance Mercury. Apollo is the artist who promotes love for everything and everyone, especially animals and Nature. Mercury represents our individual sexuality, and the two mounts combined represent sexuality shared with a partner, the intimate sexuality that we experience with a single person. Why else do we adorn the ring finger, which stems from this mount, with a ring, when we fall in love or get married?

Apollo externalizes his emotions better than any other god; and, as he was bade by Jupiter, he drives the Sun chariot which gives us light, heat and fertility when it is driven carefully, but which may bring about our own downfall if driven too hastily.

Whereas Jupiter helps us to build our own personality, with Apollo we bring it to surface and dazzle those around us, externalizing it and adorning it as best as we can. It is the mount of success, which is why on some people's hands we will find that it is crossed by a line of the same name.

This all goes to show that an ordinary-sized mount represents deep love of loveliness itself, a strong creative capacity and great chances of winning fame and honour. Yet in a prominent mount all of the above may be replaced by vanity, self-indulgence, love of luxury, extravagance and materialism; and a very shallow Mount of Apollo may be a sign of a loner, a rather lifeless person who finds life a bore.

VENUS

Some chirologists like to believe that the Mount of Venus, which is at the base of the thumb, is the third phalanx of this two-phalanxed finger (fig. IV.7). It covers almost a third of the palm and is the highest and largest mount on our hands. The goddess's best qualities are most likely to be found in a mount that is soft yet firm to the touch, a little higher than the other mounts and slightly pinkish.

The Mount of Venus rules everything and anything that is related to our family, love, children and our closest friends. The "family line" marks the frontier between the mount and the base of the thumb and gives us a cle-

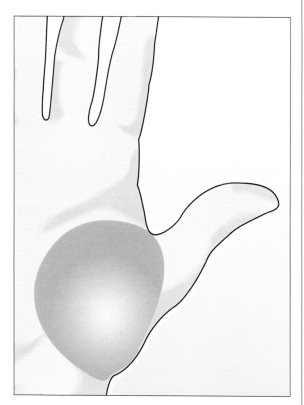

■ *Fig. IV.7. Mount of Venus. It is the most important pad of the hand, and takes up approximately three quarters of the palm.*

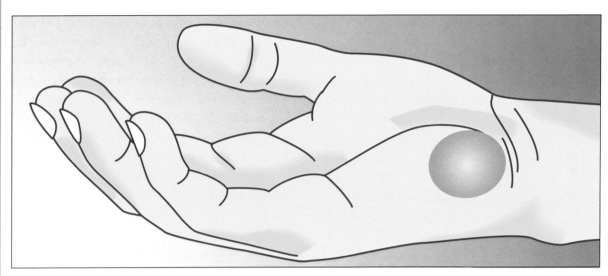

■ *Fig. IV.8. Mount of the Moon, near the wrist.*

ar idea about the state of relationships with our relatives.

Most of the mount is bordered by the life line, so it has a lot to say about our general state of health, especially the reproductive organs, kidneys, throat and ear. A close relationship also exists between the Mount of Venus and the pelvis. On a woman's hand, a wide mount is a sign of a wide pelvis so she will find it easier to give birth. Along the same lines, a narrow mount suggests difficulties at childbirth.

The relationship between Venus and Mars is highly important, because when the two come together, they give birth to their daughter, Harmony. So if you find Venus and Mars separated by lines or a deep furrow, it is quite likely that the person in question represses his or her capacity to experience pleasure. He or she is aggressive and uneasy, and makes war on anyone who freely enjoys the pleasures of life.

Broadly speaking, the Mount of Venus brings us quality, vitality, energy, capacity to love and be loved, but it can also be home to aggressiveness, brutality and an excessive appetite for sex and sensuality. Venus is our sensitive intelligence.

MOON

The Moon represents the power of the night, replacing the light of day. It is rather like a huge mirror that reflects the sunlight; therefore it has much to do with the occult and "the beyond".

It symbolizes the passive, receptive and emotional aspects of our personality. It harbours our unconscious impulses and impressions, our instincts and our imagination.

The Mount of the Moon is below Mercury and Mars, and on the opposite side to Venus (fig. IV.8). It is the home of our dreams, imagination and the desire to perceive more than the eye can see.

If the mount is too low or shallow, the individual tends to be realistic, unimaginative and boring. Such people sometimes believe that imagination is the intelligence of fools or conformists.

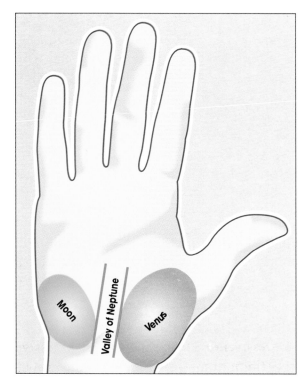

■ *Fig. IV.9. Valley of Neptune, between the Mounts of Venus and the Moon.*

NEPTUNE

The valley of Neptune is located in the middle of the palm, near the wrist and between the Mounts of Venus and the Moon (fig. IV.9). It is crossed by the life and fortune lines. When we referred to the plain of Mars, we said that this valley is the channel through which our energy flows when it enters and leaves our body. We should follow the example of Neptune by building dykes to guide and steer our energy in the right direction. If we do, we are much more likely to put our energy to good use than if we let this part of our hand remain disorganized. Our energy will be an invaluable help to us in our tasks if we give it the heart and strength of a horse, then manage to tame it.

This valley reflects our working life and how we are coping with it. Since it is the most passive area of our hand, it reveals any external factors that may be affecting us, and whether we are capable of defending ourselves (fig. IV.10).

Moreover, a valley that is firm and clearly-defined indicates a person who has charisma, heals easily and can cope with rough times. He or she can influence other people and is a good speaker.

THE GODS AND THEIR TASKS

Now that we have analyzed the personality of each god on our hands (fig. IV.11), we could summarize their roles as follows:

Saturn - The great architect, builder of our inner temple of wisdom, and the centre in which all our ideas are formed.

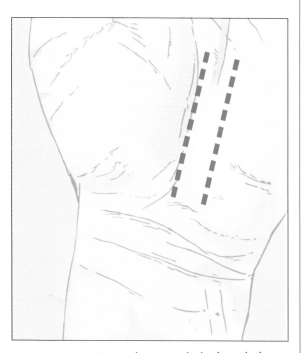

■ *Fig. IV.10. Energy leaves our body through the two channels in the Valley of Neptune.*

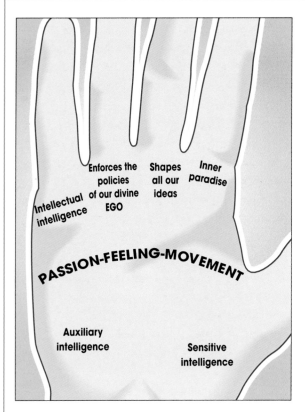

Enforces the policies of our divine **EGO**

Shapes all our ideas

Inner paradise

Intellectual intelligence

PASSION-FEELING-MOVEMENT

Auxiliary intelligence

Sensitive intelligence

■ *Fig. IV.11. Meaning of the energy capacities of each fleshy pad of our hands.*

Jupiter - The works of the gods only take shape in the material world through Jupiter. He builds our inner paradise and rouses our feelings.

Apollo - Externalizes our emotions, makes us behave as we do and enforces the policies of our divine ego.

Mercury - Is our intellectual intelligence and gives us our life script.

Mars - Receives guidelines from all the other gods and draws up a work schedule. He is the driving force behind our movements.

Venus - Is our sensitive intelligence, and she holds the secret of the conservative strength of love, and the power of intelligence and justice.

Moon - Is our auxiliary intelligence. Mercury gives it our life script, which the Moon then stages to make us understand it.

When all the work schedules are ready, energy flows in and out of us through Neptune via the wrist, which is responsible for injecting life, strength and power into these schedules, each mount having its own. Yet we alone are powerless to carry out these tasks in our material world. We need a hero, a son of the gods. And to transform our energy our hero needs channels - the fingers - that have gates, the phalanxes.

However, each phalanx is defended by a mythological guardian and since our hero's mission is to ensure that our energy comes out fresh and capable of transforming our exterior, one by one he must beat each guardian.

This hero is Hercules, and he will be the main character of the next chapter. We will use the Twelve Labours that he was given by the gods to explain and analyze the role that each finger and phalanx plays in palmistry.

CHAPTER V

THE FINGERS AND PHALANXES

T he so-called Twelve Labours of Hercules are the most symbolic, fantastic and imaginative part of mythology. Many authors have studied the subject, and some have even gone so far as to seek possible connections between the Labours of Hercules and the twelve signs of the Zodiac. Their efforts have resulted in a system of keys and symbols that makes these connections easier to interpret.

Chirologists have also sought such connections and applied them to the fingers. The thumbs, however, are so important that they require a separate study, so we will look at them later on.

Each of our ten fingers is related to one of the elements, and each phalanx of each finger is related to a different sign of the Zodiac (fig. V.1). By looking at these connections in this chapter, later on we will realize just how important fingers are in palmistry.

THE FINGERS

Index finger - Starts at the Mount of Jupiter and its element is Fire. The first phalanx is related to Gemini, the middle phalanx to Taurus and the third, and furthest from the palm, is related to Aries.

Ring finger - Starts at the Mount of Apollo and its element is Water. The phalanx nearest to the palm is related to Virgo, the middle phalanx to Leo and the last to Cancer.

Little finger - Starts at the Mount of Mercury and its element is Air. The first phalanx is related to Sagittarius, the second to Scorpio and the third to Libra.

Middle finger - Starts at the Mount of Saturn and its element is Earth. The first phalanx is related to Pisces, the second to Aquarius and the third to Capricorn.

THE LABOURS OF HERCULES

After explaining how the signs of the Zodiac are distributed, now we will talk about the

Labours of Hercules. We will look at how they are interpreted, and how they are related to the four elements, which symbolize the labours of Mankind. We will also analyze their different stages and psychological messages (fig. V.2).

The Nemean Lion.
Second phalanx of the ring finger
(fig. V.3)

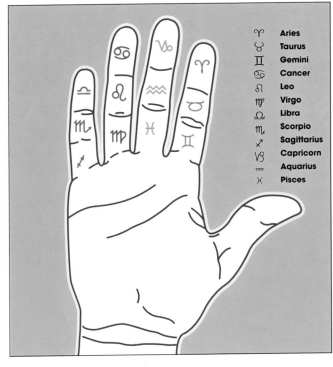

♈	Aries
♉	Taurus
♊	Gemini
♋	Cancer
♌	Leo
♍	Virgo
♎	Libra
♏	Scorpio
♐	Sagittarius
♑	Capricorn
♒	Aquarius
♓	Pisces

■ *Fig. V.1. The phalanxes of the fingers with their respective signs of the zodiac.*

The Hydra of Lerna.
First phalanx of the ring finger
(fig .V.4)

The First Labour of Hercules was to kill a monstrous lion that was devastating the region of Nemea. Symbolically, this task involves balancing Fire and Air, controlling impulse with reason, using energy with discernment, and resolution with sufficient logic. In keeping with this theory, our will-power is forged in Aries; Leo, the second fire sign, builds the inner wisdom that we need in order to create; and it is through Sagittarius, the last fire sign, that we express and display our creative talent to other people.

Each of us must fight and defeat our own Nemean Lion, which rules the middle phalanx of our ring finger. Depending on the nature of these phalanxes, it will be our balance, our capacity for initiative, energy and decision. If our skin is red or suffers anomalies (as we pointed out in the chapter on the skin) it will be a sign that our fight with the lion is a tough one, or that we are losing it.

Our hero's Second Labour was to kill the hideous Hydra which, together with an enormous crab, was devastating the lands of Lerna, near Argos, beside the River Amymone. The Hydra had nine heads, and every time that Hercules cut off one of the heads, two more heads would spring up in its place. Therefore Hercules sought the help of his nephew Iolaus. As soon as Hercules cut one of the heads, off, Iolaus burnt the neck to prevent more heads from growing. In the end Hercules managed to kill the monster and buried it.

This is the first mention of the idea of family and society helping to solve a problem. Three of the elements - water, earth and fire - are also reflected here. This is the sign of Cancer, faithfully represented by the enormous crab that attacked Hercules and by the hydra's nine heads.

It is the first water sign; the door through which feelings, desires and emotions enter our world. Man's enjoys his first taste of love in this sign; first it takes us into a few short relationships to steadily prepare our sensitivity; later on love flourishes within us and, when we are ready, we can leap towards immaterial love, shapeless love.

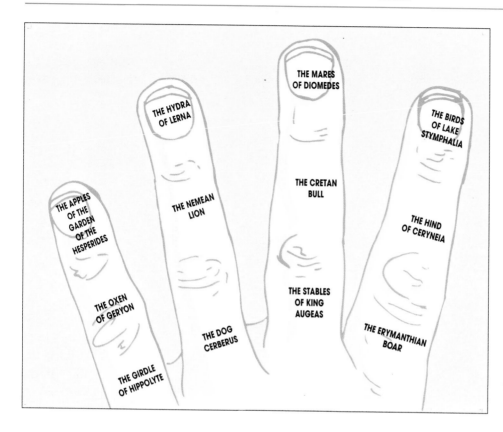

THE MARES
OF DIOMEDES

THE HYDRA
OF LERNA

THE BIRDS
OF LAKE
STYMPHALIA

THE CRETAN
BULL

THE APPLES
OF THE
GARDEN
OF THE
HESPERIDES

THE NEMEAN
LION

THE HIND
OF CERYNEIA

THE OXEN
OF GERYON

THE STABLES
OF KING
AUGEAS

THE DOG
CERBERUS

THE ERYMANTHIAN
BOAR

THE GIRDLE
OF HIPPOLYTE

■ *Fig. V.2. The phalanxes of the fingers compared to the Labours of Hercules.*

However, water has to come together, filter and flow through the Earth; it is the primordial basis of life - why else are we told that God created us from clay? But if water stays still, becomes stagnant and a home to parasites, reptiles and monsters, it will be warning us that our feelings are not evolving, that our emotions are coming to a standstill. All this gives rise to radical attitudes, and we could lose touch with reality. Our feelings could run wild, just as the hydra's heads started to multiply uncontrollably.

We should remember that our hydra protects the doors to our ring finger phalanxes that are furthest from the palm. If we look carefully at these phalanxes, we will see how desires, emotions and feelings enter our lives, how strongly we balance them and who helps us in that struggle.

The Erymanthian Boar Third phalanx of the index finger
(fig. V.5)

Hercules' Fourth Labour was to capture alive a fearsome boar that was terrorizing all the inhabitants of the region of Arcadia.

The boar represents the base instincts and fierceness that lie within us all, and we must tame if it is to be of any use to us. Our boar rules the phalanxes of the index finger that are closest to the palm, where he waits for us to discover how we are shaping our inner balance.

As always, if there is any anomaly, change of size or colour, or if this phalanx has more lines than the rest, it will be a sign of our psychological situation.

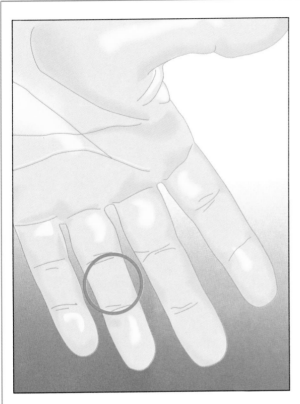

■ *Fig. V.3. The Nemean Lion (the balance between fire and air) rules the second phalanx of the ring finger.*

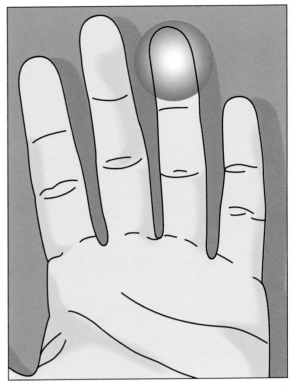

■ *Fig. V.4. The Second Labour of Hercules, in the first phalanx of the ring finger. Balance between water and earth.*

The Hind of Ceryneia.
Second phalanx of the index finger
(fig. V.6)

This hind lived on Mount Ceryneia and had been offered by one of the Pleiades to the goddess Diana as a tribute. The animal was famed for its extraordinary swiftness, its golden antlers and copper-coloured hooves. Hercules was ordered to capture it alive and take it to the temple of Mycenae.

Symbolically, now we are in Taurus, the second earth sign, where Man has been taught the mysteries of the material world. Taurus rules the middle phalanx of our index fingers; these are plots of fertile land, sown with seeds that soak up our inner humidity in a race to germinate as soon as possible.

We use our index finger to judge or accuse or point at another person, and in order for our judgment or opinion to be balanced, our finger must be straight. It must not bend or deviate. Depending on the nature of our middle phalanx, or the wisdom of our Taurus, our index finger will allow us to understand and help others, instead of making unfounded judgements. Our index finger also denotes pride and ambition. A large middle phalanx may be a sign of exaggerated selfishness in earthly matters, and a strong ambition to live a life surrounded by luxury.

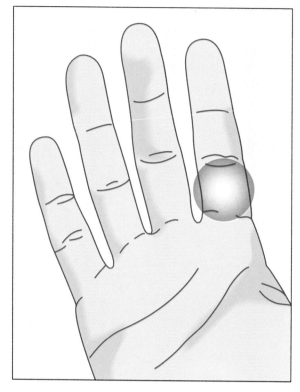

■ *Fig. V.5. The Erymanthian Boar is in the third phalanx of the index finger. It means a balance between water and fire.*

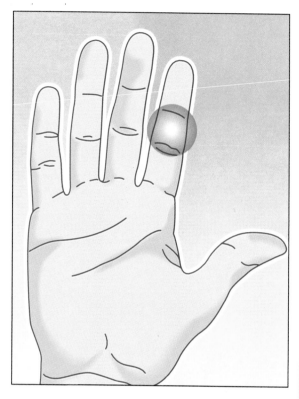

■ *Fig. V.6. The Hind of Ceryneia, in the second phalanx of the index finger, means the necessary balance between earth and water.*

The Birds of Lake Stymphalia.
First phalanx of the index finger
(fig. V.7)

The Sixth Labour of Hercules was to exterminate a flock of destructive birds that had spread like wildfire in the woods surrounding Lake Stymphalia.

This is the first sign of the Zodiac, the most individual sign of all, ruled by Mars, the warrior, the hero, the leader. This is in Aries, the sign of will, the door through which the divine enter the human realm. Even though Aries forces us to fight to defend our individuality, because society becomes unfair and heartless, we cannot afford to accept that the

collective unit is indestructible, or that there is no point in fighting its devastating force on one's own.

This Labour shows us that we must take a clear, decisive stand against mistaken social structures if we wish to see greater harmony and equilibrium in the world around us.

Our "birds" lie in the last phalanx of our index fingers, i.e., the phalanxes that are furthest from the palm. This phalanx contains the start of our life schedule, our personality, the strength we need to reach "self-made" status. We should also remember that the origins of pride and ambition are also to be found in these phalanxes.

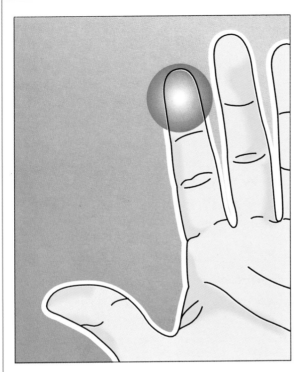

■ *Fig. V.7. The Birds of Lake Stymphalia (first phalanx of the index finger). Balance between fire and air.*

Symbolically we are in Pisces, which represents our emotional bloodstream. If Pisces is well balanced with its opposing sign Virgo, it forces us to give up material things, to settle and pay off our outstanding debts, thus enabling us to finish and learn from our experiences. This mythological labour reminds us that we must keep our interior clean, and that we should show others how clean we are, demonstrating that it is possible to be ambitious and unbiased at the same time; or that it does not matter if you get dirty, as long as you clean yourself afterwards. The danger arises if you let the dirt build up.

Our capacity for finding this balance is in our middle fingers, in the phalanx nearest the palm. The size and colour of the phalanx will show us the extent of our capacity.

The Stables of King Augeas.
Third phalanx of the middle finger
(fig. V.8)

The Fifth Labour of Hercules was to cleanse in one day the stables of King Augeas, which were in a filthy state because the King had never looked after them. No-one had ever dared to undertake such an unpleasant task, even though Augeas had offered a tenth of his riches to whoever managed to clean the stables.

Hercules made strategically-placed holes in the walls of the stables. The he diverted the course of the region's two largest rivers, the Peneius and the Alpheus, making them pass through the stables. By doing so, he managed to clean them in a single day.

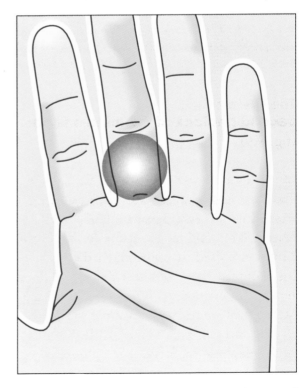

■ *Fig. V.8. The Stables of King Augeas, connected to Pisces, are in the third phalanx of the middle finger.*

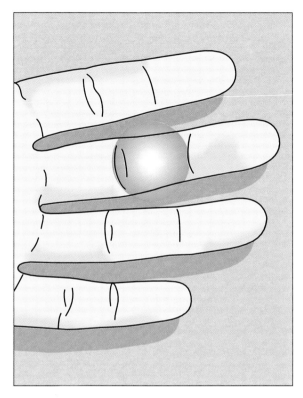

The Cretan Bull.
Second phalanx of the middle finger
(fig. V.9)

Myth has it that on the island of Crete lived a fire-breathing bull that was terrorising all the island's inhabitants. Neptune had given it to Minos, King of Crete, as a sire for his herds. Minos promised that when he had crossed all his animals, he would sacrifice the bull in honour of Neptune to thank him for the gift. When the God realized that time was passing by and Minos had still not fulfilled his promise, Neptune made the bull aggressive and savage, letting loose a real nightmare.

Once again Hercules was ordered to fight a raging animal, capture it alive and after crossing the sea, take it to Eurystheus.

However, the King of Argos did not know what to do with the bull, so he gave it to the goddess Hera, who set it free again. The bull went on the rampage again, sowing panic among the region's inhabitants. It was the hero Theseus who captured the bull the second time around. Theseus was a great friend of Hercules, and helped him complete many of his Labours.

This was the first task that Hercules failed to complete alone, because it was Theseus who finished it.

We can see that the experience Hercules gained in his previous Labours is starting to bear fruit; instead of working alone, he now relies on his friends; he lets them help him to finish the job, and appreciates and uses other people's help. Above all, he realizes that even though he can do the job well, he alone is not strong enough to dominate a beast who might be set free again at any moment. Now is the time to take a different course of action, and to contribute with our reasoned experience to foster the collective work of mankind. Now is the time for self-improvement; the time to grow and become freer and more reasonable.

Aquarius rules in the middle phalanx of our middle fingers. Therefore it is Aquarius that balances us. Saturn is the source of our middle finger, which is set against Neptune, so the middle phalanxes channel and transform the sources of inspiration and energy that flow from Neptune, and wisely use the natural and material assets supplied by Saturn. If the phalanxes are well and nicely-shaped, we will have a very good chance of improving whatever we do and, maybe, of improving our own attitudes. Therefore we will be in a position to balance our mind and make it reason properly.

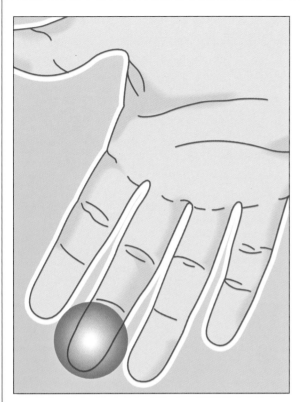

■ *Fig. V.10. The Mares of Diomedes, which correspond to the sign of Capricorn, are in the first phalanx of the middle finger.*

The Mares of Diomedes.
First phalanx of the middle finger
(fig. V.10)

The Eighth Labour of Hercules was to capture the four mares of Diomedes, King of Thrace, which ate only human flesh and attacked anyone who went near them. To capture the man-eating mares, Hercules had to fight the armies of Diomedes, defeat them and kill the King. Then he threw Diomedes' body to the mares and trapped them as they devoured their former master.

These symbolic animals eat only human flesh. They represent the four punishments that man suffers in his material life; they are the four Horsemen of the Apocalypse who constantly remind us of our existence, and whom we are powerless to fight. We can only trap them and watch over them.

These animals represent hunger, war, disease and death. They are real and sooner or later one or all four of them will devour us.

This Labour symbolizes Capricorn, the earth sign, which shows us the value of time and all the active values of the material world. Reality takes shape, but we must mark the boundaries of such reality and we do so through the god Saturn, the great builder. It is Saturn who lays down the rules that govern the powers of Nature. We need to feed, to live in our environment, to feel reality, yet must always leave aside greed, and any slavery to vices, luxury and ambition.

The phalanxes that represent this sign are in the middle fingers, or Saturn's fingers, and are furthest from the palm; these phalanxes divide and mark the balance of the other fingers. If we bring the three phalanxes together, we will see that the middle finger is home to Capricorn, who shows the time; Aquarius, who endows us with reason, and Pisces, who cleans us as thoroughly as a flood. So this is the finger where good and evil manifest themselves as a single force. What we achieve will depend on how we use that force.

The Girdle of Hippolyte.
Third phalanx of the little finger
(fig. V.11)

Hippolyte, Queen of the Amazons, always wore a beautiful golden girdle that she had been given by the god Mars, and which was the envy of all other women. One of those who coveted the girdle was Admete, daughter of Eurystheus. So Hercules' next Labour was to fetch the trophy.

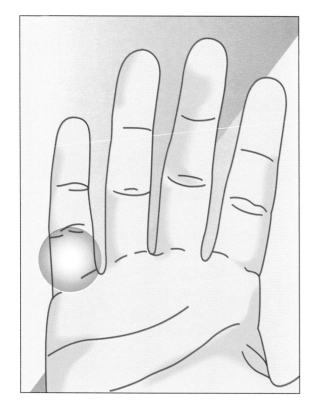

■ *Fig. V.11. The Girdle of Hippolyte, or balance bet-ween fire and air, is in the third phalanx of the little finger.*

The Amazons were a tribe of female warriors, famous for their skilful archery. They killed their male offspring and taught their daughters in the art of using weapons. Hercules managed to reach their territory, in Asia Minor, and persuaded the Queen to give him the girdle. But the goddess Juno, his eternal enemy, not content with Hercules' new triumph, came down to Earth as an Amazon. She roused the female tribe against Hercules, urging them to capture him and retrieve the girdle, so Hercules had to fight the Amazons and kill Hippolyte. In the end he managed to take by force what originally had been given to him.

This Ninth Labour represents a balance between masculinity and femininity, which

are always united by a narrow girdle, always needing both types of impulse, yet always fighting each other in a never-ending battle to obtain the power of the girdle.

Just like in Hercules' adventure, man receives from woman the gift of life by spending nine months (the ninth labour) linked to a woman by an umbilical chord, his life thus depending on this chord and on woman's devotion. However, in spite of this close relationship that exists at his birth, later on he struggles to kill the feminine part that is inside every human being, as if he wanted to hide his origins, or felt ashamed to admit who possesses the power of the girdle.

Our masculine-feminine balance lies in our little fingers, in the phalanxes nearest the

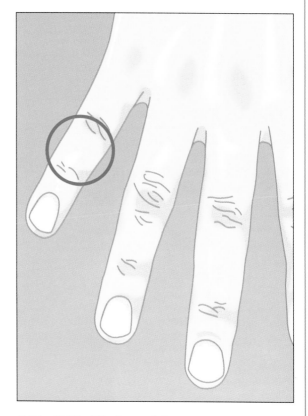

■*Fig. V.12. The Oxen of Geryon in the second phalanx of the little finger, or Scorpio.*

palm, just above Mercury. It is here that the intellect offers Man the chance of seeking a shared sexuality, not one of dominion or slavery; where we learns how to use diplomacy to solve our problems, instead of brute force. In short, it is here that we can write the script of the life that we would like to lead. When the phalanx is adorned with rings (with Hippolyte's girdle), we may unconsciously be indicating that Hercules' battle with the Amazons represents the constant struggle of our lives.

The Oxen of Geryon.
Second phalanx of the little finger
(fig. V.12)

The Tenth Labour of Hercules consisted of stealing the cattle of the monstrous Geryon, a three-headed and three-bodied giant who lived on the island of Erythia, and who guarded a flock of cattle aided by the herdsman Eurytion and the two-headed dog Orthrus.

Our hero reached Libya, where he fought and killed the giant Anteus, then passed through the Strait of Gibraltar, where he built the Pillars of Hercules to mark the boundaries of the known world. He had to kill the two-headed dog, which symbolizes the need for Man to assume duality: good and evil, masculinity and femininity, the right and left hemispheres of the brain; in a word, Man must understand the need for unity, that one pole cannot exist without the other, try as hard as he might to deny this fact. In theory the idea seems very easy to understand and share, yet in practice very few people eventually manage to see just how incomplete human beings would be with only one of the two poles.

This Labour takes us to the sign of Scorpio, the second water sign. Scorpio lets

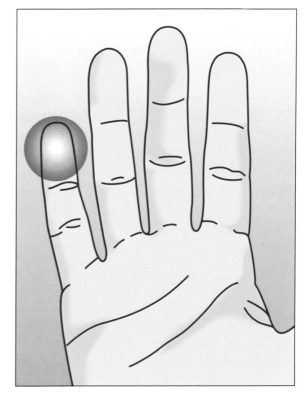

■ *Fig. V.13. The Apples of the Garden of the Hesperides in the first phalanx of the little finger.*

emotions reach our interior, where they take root and endeavour to balance their counterpart Taurus, the earth sign. They strive to make us set aside power and riches and instead make work and serving other people our goal.

Scorpio rules the middle phalanx of our little fingers. Earlier on we pointed out that the lower phalanx is ruled by Sagittarius, which also suggests the idea of polarity; and that our little finger, which is ruled by Mercury, the most polyvalent god, is home to our intellectual world and sexuality. So we must look at this finger and its phalanxes very carefully, because the less balanced their shape, the steeper and rougher we will find the path towards understanding.

The Apples of the Garden of the Hesperides.
First phalanx of the little finger
(fig. V.13)

The Eleventh Labour of Hercules was to fetch the golden apples that grew in a hidden garden, famous for its beauty. Legend had it that the garden was looked after by the three Hesperides nymphs, daughters of Atlas and Hesperida, and guarded by Ladon, a hundred-headed dragon that never slept.

Hercules left for the north, and the nymphs of the River Eridanus told him that the sea-god Nereus knew where the garden was. Hercules fought and defeated Nereus, who revealed to him that Prometheus was the only person who knew where the apples were; yet Prometheus was chained to the highest summit of Mount Caucasus, tortured by an eagle that continuously picked at his liver. Hercules went to Prometheus, freed him and killed the eagle. In return, Prometheus told him how to reach the garden, and warned him that the only person who could enter the garden was Atlas, the father of the Hesperides.

Atlas was the giant who had been condemned to hold up the sky on his shoulders, so Hercules told the giant that if he brought him the apples, he would carry Atlas' heavy burden for him forever. But once the giant had returned with the golden apples, Hercules tricked him and left with the apples.

The story shows that Man, just like Hercules, is bound to investigate, interrogate, fight and travel if he wishes to reach the divine fruit. Hercules found that he was there was nothing he could do unless he joined forces with others in his quest for the truth. He had to understand and respect the divine laws, and was even forced to hold up the sky. This is like

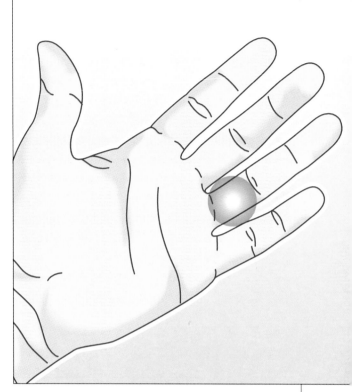

■ *Fig. V.14. The Dog Cerberus. Third phalanx of the ring finger.*

admitting that if we fail to heed the laws of the Universe, everything could collapse around us.

This is the sign of Libra, the entrance through which the cosmic energies enter Man. It is the sign of justice, harmony, association and team-work, where the individual finds the thread that can help him unravel the truth.

Libra rules the phalanx that is furthest from the palm, so now we have seen the three sections of the little finger, which plays such an important role. Further importance must be attached to this phalanx because its characteristics will indicate the nature of our patient's ideas.

The Dog Cerberus.
Third phalanx of the ring finger

(fig. V.14)

The last and Twelfth Labour of Hercules was the hardest and most complicated, because Eurystheus ordered Hercules to go down to the Underworld and capture alive Cerberus, a monstrous dog that stood guard at the gate of Avernus. Hercules sought the help of Mercury, who was responsible for accompanying the souls of the dead to the Underworld. Mercury initiated Hercules in the Elysian mysteries, which revealed how to reach the world of the dead. When Hercules reached the Underworld, he came across his friend Theseus, and rescued him from the clutches of death; then he asked Pluto, the god of the Underworld, for permission to fight Cerberus. Pluto let him, as long as he used only his bare hands as weapons. Hercules seized the monsters's three heads at the same time, and struggle as hard as it might, the animal was unable to free itself from the hero's tight grasp, and eventually gave in.

Having completed this Labour, Hercules was now free and won the immortality that he had been promised.

This phalanx is ruled by Virgo, the third earth sign and the last sign of the Zodiac. Now it is time to settle accounts, the chance to discard earthly things; the time to make use of the skills we have gained so far from experience. We must talk to the god of the Underworld, and ask him to let us conquer the guardian of our nightmares because now we can master them. It is the time to ask Mercury to show us how to overcome our tortures and embark on the voyage to real freedom.

The sign of Virgo is in our ring finger, and rules the phalanx closest to the palm. As we said when we referred to Apollo, when we get engaged to someone, we wear a ring on this phalanx to show everyone our commitment and signal that we are starting a new life. In the same way, it marks a new stage in the Labours of Hercules, who must now employ the experience he has gained through fire, water and air in any situations that he may meet from now on. The same goes for us.

Phalanx by phalanx, we have now looked at each of the mental activities that are represented by each of the fingers. Now we are better placed to summarize or synthesize the personality of each finger, although we must remember the support that each finger receives from its respective Mount-God, and the three Labours that it is capable of performing. Nevertheless, we have yet to discuss the human being's most important finger, the one that sets us apart from other animals because it allows us to perform tasks that call for precision. This finger stands out from the rest, and police all over the world use it to identify us. In the words of Newton, this finger "was man". All religions identify it with their God. In short, we are talking about the thumb.

THE THUMB

Throughout the chapter we have looked at the different psychological tasks that Man must face and cannot avoid. One by one, they are detailed on each phalanx of our hands.

In the previous chapter we described the personalized centres that contain the energy we need for each task. These centres are known by the name of a god and are located on a swelling or fleshy depression on the palm of our hands. However, the hand is incomplete, because the most important finger is still to come: the thumb (fig. V.15). This is home to the reasoned will, logic and firmness that let us choose our own path, confronting our own feelings or instincts if need be.

After having explored the inner world of the rest of the hand, a study of the thumb will convince us that over and above heroes and gods there lies a single energy, a principle, a single God from whom all of us spring forth and to whom all of us will return. It is like repeating the famous saying of Newton, the founder of modern physics: "If there was no other proof, the thumb would convince that God exists".

At the base of this finger is Venus, the Mount that takes up a third of the whole palm of the hand. As we saw in the previous chapter, in Man the goddess Venus is the centre of all feelings of love. She steers the human being towards his fellow men.

Moreover, of all the gods, Venus was the only one who was born from the sea, after it had been fertilized by the virile member of Uranus, which fell into the sea when it was cut off by Saturn. She is also the goddess who enjoys men's company and even falls in love with some of them. All these features make the thumb a special finger that must remain separate from the others if it is to work in opposite directions to them.

It is the finger that frees us, and will be the key to mental healing the day that psychology adopts it as a technique, and finds that it is the only finger capable of rescuing us from the obscure world of nightmares. We should remember that only the thumb is in a position to fight, as our hero Hercules did, all the monsters that live in the twelve phalanxes of the other fingers. Only the thumb is invincible, though sometimes we feel trapped by some of the monsters.

Will, logic and reasoning are the human being's most essential weapons, and together they are strong enough to overcome any situation, however difficult or serious it may seem. That is why people who are very pessimistic, depressive or suffer mental problems tend to hide their thumbs inside a closed fist. If we can persuade them to give up the habit and not hide their thumbs, their state of mind will improve considerably.

This habit of hiding our thumb is also common at birth and when we are about to die, because it indicates the fear that is taking over us, forcing us to cover our willpower with our other fingers. Different clinical studies have shown that this position of the thumb is very frequent in epileptic fits.

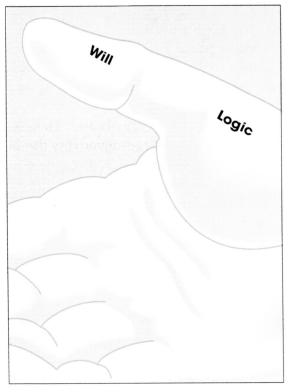

■ *Fig. V.15. The thumb: the finger that sets us apart from all other animals. The first phalanx is home to will, and the second to logic.*

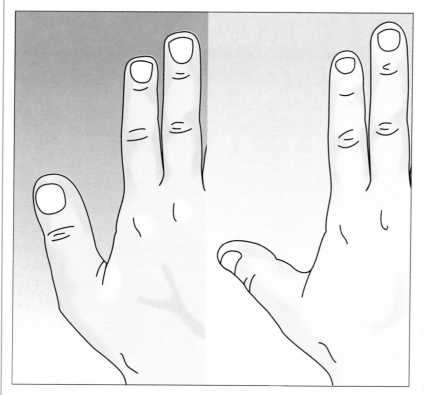

■ *Fig. V.16. Left: thumb in line with the other fingers –people with little control of their own will. Right: thumb set apart from the other fingers– a sign of self-control.*

The thumb has only two phalanxes, so it is a single force with two tendencies; the spiritual world joins the material world, will and energy join logic and reason. Reasoning air stokes our creative fire. Therefore we can lean a lot about someone just by looking at their thumb.

The phalanx closest to the palm of the hand is ruled by logic and reason, but also has much to do with the material realm. If it is the largest phalanx of the thumb, our client is endowed with judgment and wisdom: However, he is very much attached to material goods and his willpower is likely to be more theoretical than real.

If, on the other hand, your largest phalanx is the one furthest from your palm, your willpower will rule over understanding. You are a

very spiritual person, with a great and noble spirit.

A long thumb affirms one's personality and is a source of reasoned decision and energy; but if it is unusually long it could be a sign of stubbornness, despotism and a tendency to tyrannize other people. Whereas a short-thumbed person feels more at home with feelings than with ideas, some chirologists think that a short thumb is ruled by the heart. However, if it is too short the person in question may have no initiative whatsoever, no willpower and be condemned always to obeying everyone else.

The thumb's position of rotation also plays a highly important role in interpreting. Hold out your hand. If your thumb is in line with your other fingers, so that you can see the five fingernails on the back (fig V.16, left), it means that your will is no match for desire, and you readily accept other people's suggestions and opinions.

If, however, your thumb is set apart from the other fingers and, at most, you can see a third of the fingernail on the back of the hand (fig. V.16, right), it is a sign of self-control, that you are determined to be your own boss, not through a feeling of guilt but of self-respect.

The thumb is also home to the sense of family duty, and any problems derived from cohabitation. As an example I will describe a case involving a couple of newlyweds, whom I call Michael and Chantal.

They knew that I was interested in chirology, so with a mix of concern and amused curiosity they told me that both of them had accidentally cut the thumb of their right hand, though only slightly. However, Michael had cut the phalanx furthest from his palm while Chantal had cut the one closest to her palm. They had no qualms about asking me if the cuts meant

RING
Love

MIDDLE
Wisdom

INDEX
Ambition

LITTLE
Diplomacy

THUMB
Will

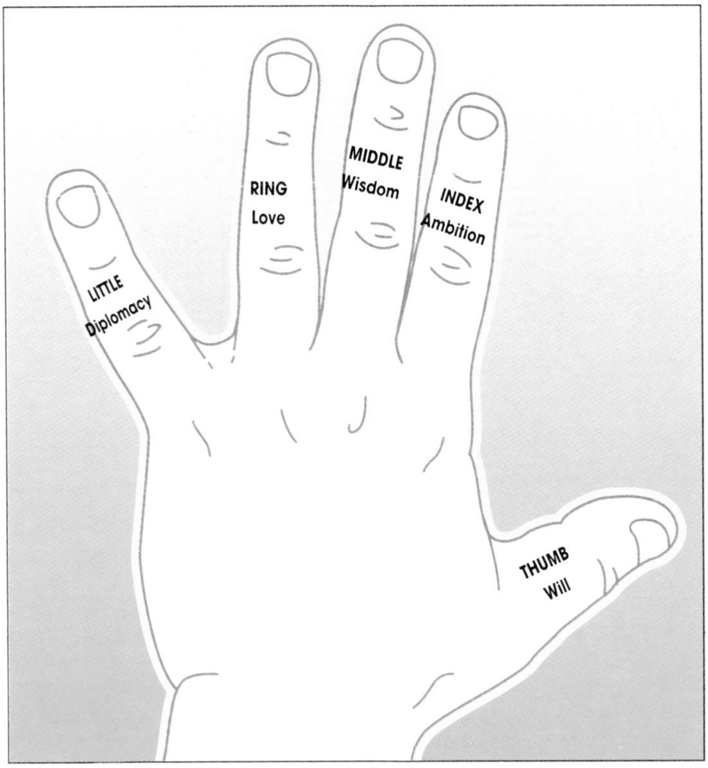

■ *Fig. V.17. We can analyze pride by our index finger; wisdom, by our middle finger; love, by our ring finger and diplomacy, by the little finger. The thumb reminds us of rationality, giving us will, logic, reason and feelings.*

band, and did not want to have to share him with his relatives. She was also considering the material issues: as they had to pay for the trip to see his family, very probably they would not have enough money to spend a few days somewhere else. Therefore she had cut her more material phalanx, the one nearest the palm.

The shape of someone's thumb can also reveal much about their basic

anything. Michael was planning to visit his relatives, who lived abroad, and when I looked at their hands I realized that the trip had caused a minor confrontation between them. The location of their cuts showed what each one thought and felt. Michael wanted to go on the trip, and had already prepared it. Yet in doing so he had denied himself the chance of enjoying himself much more elsewhere with his wife, free of any family obligations. So his sense of duty and his desire to keep his relatives happy had overruled his logic. He had cut himself on his willpower phalanx.

Chantal, on the other hand, was using logic and reason. Since her feelings for Michael's family were not as strong as his, she obviously wanted to go on the trip alone with her hus-

psychology, because it receives impulses from the nervous system more quickly and easily than the other fingers, and it is the first to betray our deepest emotions.

First we will look at the most noticeable –and negative– type of thumb, which luckily is not seen too often: the ball thumb, also known as "club thumb" or "murderer's" thumb. In this type of thumb, the phalanx furthest from the palm is ball-shaped. To the minds of many chirologists, cave men must have had this type of thumb because it is the typical thumb of impulsive, thoughtless, very aggressive and violent people. Moreover, if the lower phalanx is very short, the individual in question may have a savage, bad-tempered streak that could reach the point of murder.

However, if the rest of his hand reveals positive features he will only resort to shouting as a form of self-defence, and anyone who shouts louder than him will get the upper hand. As a matter of fact, these people are ruled by anger, and do not meditate or think over their actions; they simply get carried away by their anger, which is their sole defence mechanism. So the more slender, balanced and lovely this finger is, the more imaginative, resourceful and reasonable the person will be.

If we listed the skills and abilities of our fingers, we would realize that some provide ideas, theory or ideals, whereas others are practical, reasonable and energetic. If we divide the hand lengthways through the middle finger, the thumb side of our hand would be our more real part and the little finger side the more imaginative part. Each finger would have the following characteristics (fig. V.17):

Index - Ambition, pride, honour, devotion, anger.
Middle - Prudence, wisdom, pessimism, fatality, melancholy.
Ring - Love, resourcefulness, success, happiness, spirit, art.
Little - Diplomacy, commerce, science, sexuality.
Thumb - Willpower, feelings, logic and reason.

If one or several fingers lean towards another, it indicates an interest in the powers of that particular finger; i.e., if they lean towards the middle finger, the person is anxiously seeking balance and wisdom; if they lean towards the index, he wants to strengthen his personality in order to be a winner. Yet if they lean towards the ring finger, he is striving for love or success; and if they bend towards the little finger, the tendency is towards diplomacy or sex.

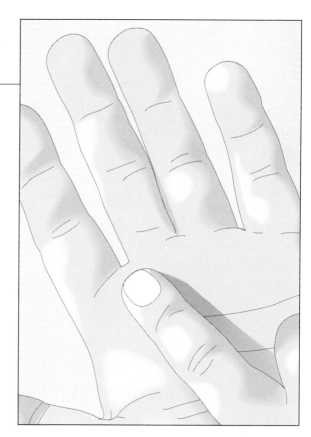

■ *Fig. V.18. When the curve of the base of our fingers forms a natural curve, it means balance.*

Broadly speaking, long fingers denote people who are meticulous and love going into detail, while short fingers denote impulsive, impetuous people; thick fingers are characteristic of people who repress their feelings and are fond the pleasures of life, whereas thin-fingered people are sensitive and express their feelings.

The base of our fingers also prompt different interpretations that are essential in unravelling someone's psychology. First of all we will analyze the arches or curve formed by the base of the fingers on the palm; secondly, the space between the bases of the fingers.

The most natural curve is the one formed when the arch is very smooth and the top, slightly higher, is between the Mounts of Saturn and Apollo. This indicates balance and harmony (fig. V.18).

If the curve is very steep because the fingers start very low down, or because the fingers seem deep-set, it denotes inferiority complexes typical of this type of hand (fig. V.19).

If there is no curve because the bases of the fingers form a straight line, it means that you are too self-confident; you trust blindly in your own judgements, without listening to other people's opinions (fig. V.20).

The spaces between the fingers give independence and confidence; the wider the space, the more outgoing and better at communicating the person will be. On the other hand, very little space, or fingers that seem to be glued to each other are a sign of great reserve, precaution, a lack of spontaneity and dependence.

The space between the Mounts of Jupiter and Saturn produces an independent mind. (See the different mounts of the hand in fig. IV.1 in the previous chapter).

The space between Saturn and Apollo provides independence from external factors and circumstances.

The space between Apollo and Mercury suggests independence of behaviour.

And, finally, total independence depends on how far you can separate the thumb and Jupiter's finger.

SHAPES OF THE FINGERTIPS

Let's imagine that our hands are plants or trees: our wrists are the roots, our palm is the trunk, and our fingers are the branches and leaves. Logically, like plants we nourish ourselves through our roots and leaves. From our roots we get what we bring with us at birth, the deepest heritage of our family genes, man's most ancient memory, the wisdom of our forefathers and the culture of our race. In a word, we draw what we need to evolve from our own fertile earth. With our branches and leaves (the fingers) we seek out the light, the sun, the air, the cleansing rain, anything new, evolution, the ideas that could forge a new mankind. Our fingers yearn to grow and reach up to touch the sky with their tips. That is precisely why the shapes of our fingertips are so important (fig. V.21). The shapes are as follows:

Conical fingertips - Also called "intuitive fingertips". They provide ideas and swiftness of thought. These people are witty, ingenious and great talkers.

Square fingertips - Also called "organized fingertips". They process everything they receive before taking it to the brain. These

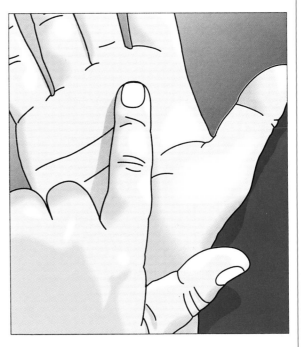

■ *Fig. V.19. A mound or depression at the base of the fingers may indicate personality complexes.*

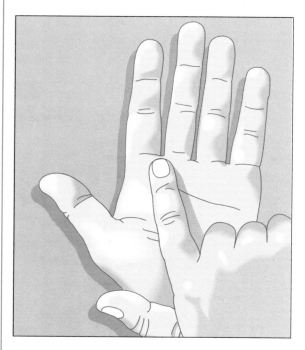

■ *Fig. V.20. If the bases of our fingers form a straight line, with no arch, we may be too self-confident.*

people are good organizers, balanced and have good visual perception.

Spatular fingertips - Also called "energetic fingertips". They give great work capacity, and are a sign of good craftsmen and people who enjoy working with their hands.

Continuing with the hand-tree simile, we know that some plants are flexible and sway in the wind. Some even use the wind to transport their seeds to other plants, forming a lovely association that prevents the air from damaging or breaking it. We could say that they dance and enjoy the wind. Similarly, flexible fingers with flexible phalanxes accept new ideas and consider them, instead of rejecting them. Yet they are incapable of doing only one thing at a time, and readily take orders from others. They are impressionable, and unpredictable in their acts and feelings. Finally, if their thumb is also flexible, their

generosity could mean that anyone can take advantage of them.

Yet other plants are stiff, inflexible and arrogantly cleave the wind in a struggle in which they would prefer to die before surrendering. They have a hardy spirit and ligneous body; they stand up to all the elements, without surrendering or making pacts with any. Similarly, by nature stiff fingers do not accept new ideas. Such people are headstrong and wary; they like secrets and do not share their feelings or problems with other people. They have a very rigid character, although they are very responsible and work hard to the very end.

The joints of our phalanxes also resemble the knots of trees. They are a good place to stop a while in order to hold an idea, take it in, digest and organize it. Once the idea is ready, it moves onto the next phalanx, where the same process takes place.

THE FINGERNAILS

It was through the fingernails that medical science first discovered how to detect endocrinal disorders, anaemia, circulatory problems and other illnesses. However, the shape, colour and consistency of fingernails also afford lots of information about their owner.

Our fingernails are one of the first tissues to grow, and appear more or less during the ninth week of pregnancy. A colony of cells form the root, which remains hidden between the skin and the flesh of the first phalanx of the finger, while other cells are responsible for forming the nerve and capillary endings and pushing out the corneous part. New fingernails grow approximately every six months.

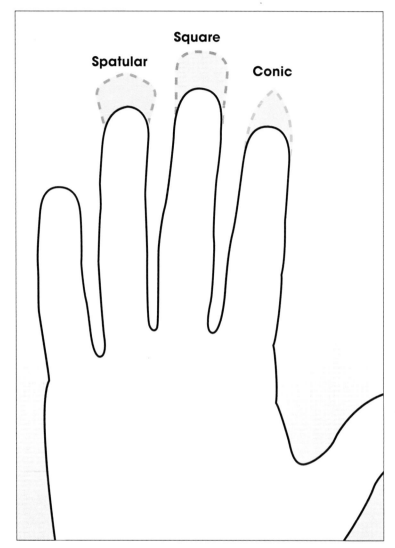

■ *Fig. V.21. How we receive or express ideas will depend on the shape of our fingertips.*

and to what extent we need to defend ourselves.

If we had to define the perfect fingernail, it would be pinkish or rosy, blending in with the rest of the hand. It should measure half the total length of the phalanx, from the cuticle to where it leaves the flesh, at the end of the finger. Square or rectangular, with parallel sides and clearly-defined curves, its length a fifth of the total size of the nail, and milky-coloured, the ideal fingernail should be shiny, and smooth to the touch. Even so, there are many types of fingernails that do not resemble this at all, and each type conveys a different message. Be that as it may, this "perfect fingernail" is a reflection of someone who possesses a strong, balanced health, a reasonable, controlled temperament, and a broad vision of the world with clear ideas. It is a healthy, harmonious fingernail.

Since fingernails are semi-transparent, we can get the first information from their colour. Reddish nails are a sign of a strong bloodstream, a tendency to hypertension and, therefore, to get overexcited and suffer fits of anger. These types of people should try to channel their anger in other directions, freeing their aggressiveness by practising sports or other energetic activities.

Bluish fingernails are a sign of poor circulation, meaning that the person probably does not let his either his feelings or blood flow freely. He seems cold and distant, although there is pent-up passion inside him, struggling to get out.

Our fingernails are made of keratin, a chemical substance. Keratin gives them the corneous nature that helps them to protect the phalanxes at the ends of our fingers. It lets our hands scratch, scrape, and do jobs that require strength, precision and detail and which would be impossible otherwise. On a physical level, our fingernails defend us; as far as our character is concerned, their shape, constitution, colour and size show us what we are like

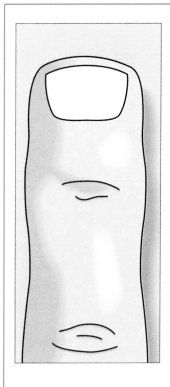

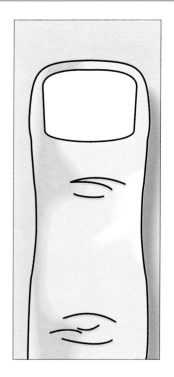

■ *Fig. V.22. Small fingernail: sign of a quarrelsome, critical and impatient nature.*

■ *Fig. V.23. Wide fingernail: loads of energy.*

Pale fingernails are a sign of weak vitality and poor nourishment; these are people who do not express their anger, but always remember any offense they have been caused; forgiveness is not one of their best virtues.

Yellowish or brownish fingernails may be a sign of liver problems or constipation. The person in question is striving to rid himself of negative emotional patterns from the past. He is trying to hold onto past problems that he should have digested, mistakenly believing that he can still find solutions; yet he has not forgotten the negative parts, which he should have erased a long time ago.

White spots on fingernails denote a loss of minerals caused by stress and anxiety. They may also be a sign of a depression that must be stopped before it gets worse.

Due to their size, small fingernails (fig. V.22) are not at all good for attacking with. Therefore the individual will constantly need to defend himself, and will be quarrelsome, critical and impatient. People who have this type of fingernail are liable to depressions and nerve or heart problems.

Wide fingernails (fig. V.23) are a sign of large amounts of energy, so these people never display malice, though at times they may express anger.

Fan-shaped fingernails (fig. V.24) and long, narrow fingernails, otherwise known as hazelnut fingernails, (fig. V.25) reveal a deficiency at the root. These people tend not to use all their energy, preferring to avoid unpleasant emotions so as not to wear themselves out. They can't stand feeling frustrated and are usually in a bad mood.

Almond-shaped fingernails (fig. V.26)

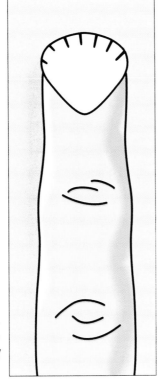

■ *Fig. V.24. Fan-shaped fingernail: tendency to avoid unpleasant emotions.*

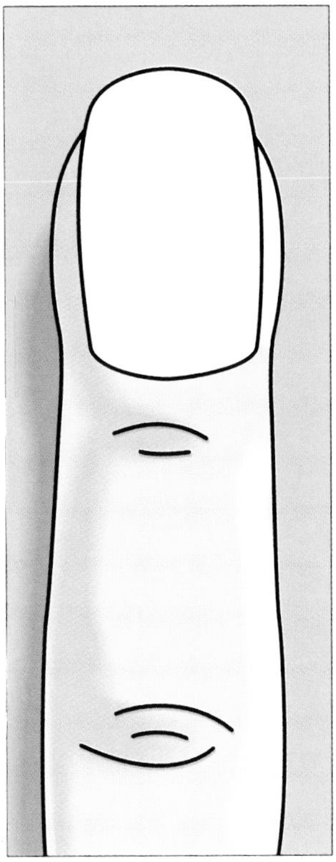

■ *Fig. V.25. If a finger is small and very long, the hazel-nut-shaped finger-nail stimulates a bad temper.*

indicate a generous, open nature, and some-one who is capable of making sacrifices for others. Such a person may lose their temper slightly, but they have such a mild nature that they never fly into a rage. This is the fin-gernail that writers and painters admire most.

Hard, narrow fingernails (fig. V.27) that grow like claws are a sign of relentless, gras-ping individuals; although they may seem charming seducers at first sight, deep down they are extremely possessive. In olden days, this fingernail was considered typical of misers and cowards.

Lastly we come to popular wisdom. Different parts of the body are attributed dif-ferent characteristics and properties by diffe-rent cultures and languages. Spanish, for example, has coined many a phrase involving fingernails. One such saying is: "Long nails, long life", which suggests that there is rela-tionship between the size of our nails and our state of health. Or if someone says you have "long fingernails", they mean you are "light-fingered", i.e. you are good at taking objects or money without other people realizing and a possible inclination to robbery.

The fact that we need our fingernails to protect our fingers could be borne out by the Spanish saying "*ser uña y carne*" which literally translates as "to be nail and flesh" and means "inseparable" or "hand in glove". In other words, anything that is or should be united.

When the Spanish say that someone is about to "*sacar las uñas*", it means they are about to "show their claws". Our fingernails can be an aggressive weapon that we can use whenever we want.

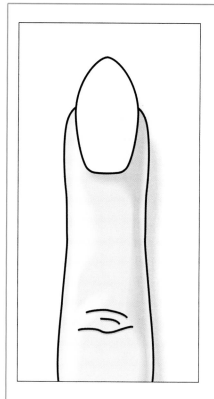

■ *Fig. V.26. Almond-shaped fingernail, much admired by writers and painters.*

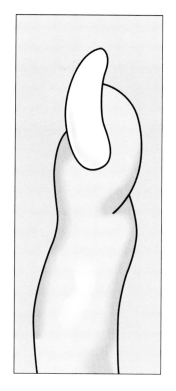

■ *Fig. V.27. Claw-type fingernail, relentless tendency to grasp and seize everything without showing any kind of emotion.*

Another saying is "*Por la uña[1] se conoce al león*", a literal translation of which would be "You can tell a lion by its claws". What it means is that you can tell how aggressive someone is by looking at their fingernails.

Last but not least, the last saying emphasizes how far we should rely on the messages that our fingernails convey: "*Uñas de gato y cara de beato*" could be rendered as "To have a cat's claws and a saint's face". No further explanation is required.

---

[1] *Inter alia*, the word «uña» means fingernail, toenail and claw. [Translator].

CHAPTER VI

LINES ON THE HAND

I n previous chapters we have studied the hand as a whole, its inner structure, and what lies beneath the skin. From this chapter on, we will be taking a look at what can be seen on the surface and what is printed on our hands. First we will deal with lines.

The great majority of treatises on chirology insist on giving the lines names and specific meanings. They even detail their possible paths across our hands, for the purpose of helping the readers to understand the relation between the lines and the development of a person's experiences.

This way of organizing their different meanings may be very necessary at first but can lead the novice chirologist to be trapped by determinism and the belief that, in many cases, his life must inevitably take the path sketched out for him since birth. He may even think that, do what he may, he cannot escape the experiences that life has in store for him and which are marked on his hands like a punishment from heaven.

Furthermore, by giving each line a particular name and meaning we may be limiting the infinite possibilities of interpretation that it has. We may even go so far as to deny the creative side we all have and which has made it possible for people over the centuries to give infinite interpretations to the same event. By studying it from different angles, in time we acquire a wealth of meanings which take us nearer to a true understanding of the event in question.

In no way do I wish to disparage the practice of allotting names and meanings to the different lines but it is important to realize that once we have learnt these concepts they must remain in the background and not become inflexible. Our hands are alive and

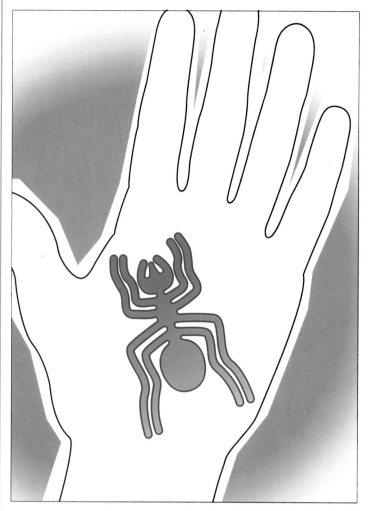

same city, but each person will give a different meaning and purpose to their journey, depending on their culture, their roots and their experiences. And it is also true that, although the city will be in the same place for all of us, we are free to go there or not, taking one route or another, going a roundabout way or straight there. Why can we not just choose the way as we go along?

In other chapters we saw how our minds are reflected in the marks on our hands, and that there is a correlation between certain areas of our hands and our brains. Therefore, we can accurately divide the hands into small, well-defined areas, according to the mental impulses that they represent.

Following this theory, the lines are communication cables between these areas. They transmit our brain's messages and act as the personal, secret code that links our conscious and our subconscious, our active and passive minds, our interior and our exterior. It shows the naked truth, as opposed to the half truth that our words tend to hide.

A sound interpretation of the lines faithfully reflects our thoughts and feelings and shows us the road that we should take.

If we decide to embark on the adventure of investigating our best means of personal development through studying the lines on our hands, we should imagine that our palm is like the mysterious Nazca lines in Peru (fig. VI.1). If we walk around them we will

our lines are too. Therefore, their meaning is equally alive and subject to the present moment, which in turn is the result of the past and will give rise to our future. It is as if we were to compare one of the three longest and deepest on our hands to a highway. It is true that the highway will always lead to the same place, but do we all need to get there in the same way? Do we all have the same reason for travelling along it?

Without a doubt it will lead us all to the

see a meaningless maze of intersecting pathways, giving no hint as to who made them or for what purpose. It is like a gigantic spider's web that defies the passing of time and continues to challenge man to discover its secrets. However, when seen from the air, the lines or paths that meant nothing to us from ground level now join together to make shapes and drawings. Although their meaning is a mystery to us, it is obvious that they are not an accident of nature and that whoever made them had a clear idea of perspective, design and art.

Just like the author of the Nazca lines, our minds use lines to tell us which way we should go, when we should rest, when danger awaits us, who accompanies us on this adventure and what weapons we should use in our daily battle. All we must do is to follow the threads of the spider's web one by one. However, from time to time, we too should take a ride in the aeroplane of our imagination. We should look down at the pattern the threads are making and which will eventually form the picture of the path we have trodden below.

Once we have accepted that our hands are a photocopy of our minds in accordance with the correlations we have established, and if we know how to follow the lines and see where they are leading to, then all that remains for us to do is to juggle all these concepts. In this way and

without realizing it, we will begin to see deep into our souls and learn that we are always free to choose our destiny.

Chirology reveals the hidden face of man; the facet that carries the seed of a wonderful being for whom neither time nor space, nor even personal limitations exist. We need only find this seed and make it grow for our lives to change and become more complete.

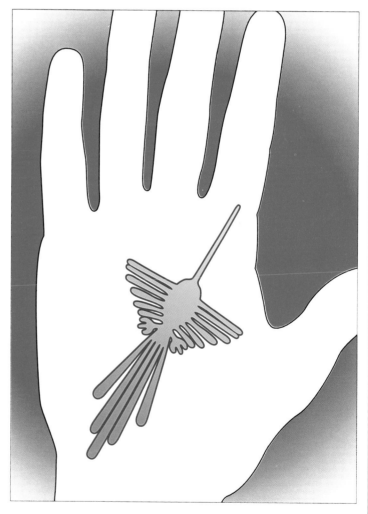

■ *Fig. VI.2. The lines on our hands make fanciful drawings.*

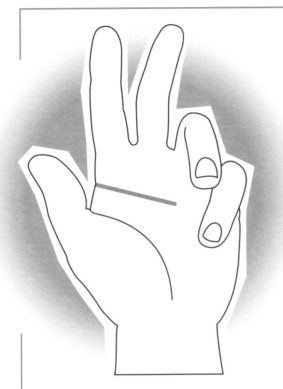

ves or forms an arch it indicates slowness, roundabout routes, weakness or slight changes (fig. VI.4). It is like taking a detour instead of the most direct route.

On the other hand, if the line is broken up it indicates insecurity or important changes. It is as if we are not sure where we want to go. It can also be telling us that the circumstances surrounding the event in question will cause us to interrupt our journey until we feel surer (fig. VI.5).

If the line is ragged it shows dispersion, lack of strength, total indecision and dreaming. The latter refers to daydreams and not to those driving forces which lead people on to great discoveries. We give ourselves up to the passive sport of daydreaming purely for entertainment or because we

The lines on our hands are the most direct link we have with our experiences. Separately or all together, they give the most reliable reading. They are the foundation stone of chirology and the chirologist's accuracy depends on their correct interpretation. This part is the easiest and most reliable, especially if we remember to apply simple, everyday interpretations to the lines. For example, straight is used to mean honest, whilst bent or twisted imply that someone's behaviour lies outside normal limits.

Therefore, if the line on our hand is straight, it shows integrity, speed of action and an iron will. The experience, message or person which our brain connects with that line will not be turned aside by anyone or anything (fig. VI.3). However, if the line cur-

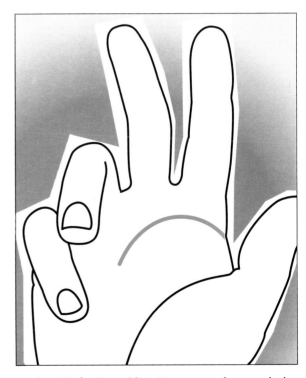

■ *Fig. VI.4. Curved line. Deviations, slowness, doubts.*

■ *Fig. VI.5. Jagged line. Sudden changes. insecurity.*

freedom and happiness. A pure, brilliant white will increase the strength of these meanings.

The deeper a line is, the more transcendence, importance and feeling it reveals. Lighter lines are less important or carry fewer meanings. Above all we must not forget the points at which each line starts and finishes and the places it passes through if we wish to reach a correct interpretation. We can read the line from beginning to end or vice versa, as we wish. We should also remember that lines can form drawings together or join up at certain points, and that all this must be deciphered.

Therefore, the same line can give rise to

know that these dreams can never come true (fig. VI.6).

As part of the general interpretation of the lines of the hand, we should bear in mind their depth and colour. Red always suggests temperament, strength and heat, so when one or more lines are redder than the rest it indicates worries, difficulties, suffering, hardships, obligations, inconveniences and anxiety. The redder the lines and the area around them, the stronger their meaning, particularly when their colour deepens and takes on a purple hue.

Lines that are whiter than the rest denote tranquillity, comfort, facility, pleasure, gaiety,

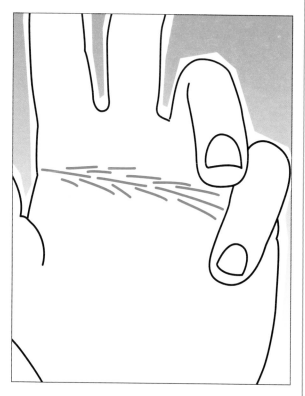

■ *Fig. VI.6. Broken-up line. Dispersion, loss of energy.*

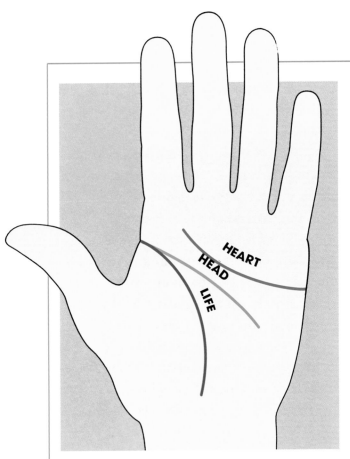

■ *Fig. VI.7. Major lines. Life line, heart line and head line.*

various readings. We could say that a line is like an actor who can take on any role when the script calls for it.

In other words, a line should never be ignored just because it has already been used in relation to some experience in a person's life. It may not be the protagonist of other experiences but it may have a secondary role to play, in which case we will have to interpret it afresh. And although I am not keen on giving lines names in case it leads to a limited conception of them, nevertheless, I have no choice but to outline the major lines on the hand and, also, some minor ones. These latter may not be present on some hands but when they

are, they have a characteristic meaning which aids our reading considerably.

MAJOR LINES

There are three major lines: the life line, the head line and the heart line (fig. VI.7). As we have said before, these three lines appear on everybody's hands, although in some cases the heart line merges with the head line, giving

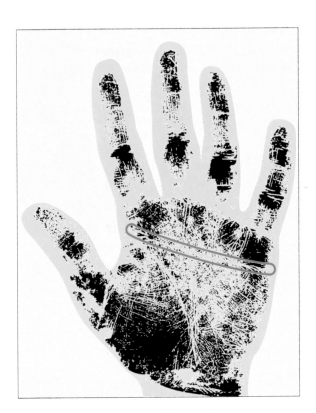

■ *Fig. VI.8. Simian line. Characteristic of people with Down's syndrome, although also found in perfectly healthy people.*

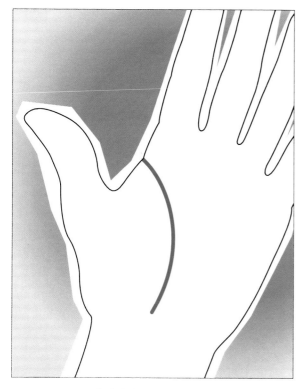

■ *Fig. VI.9. The life line begins between the index finger and thumb, skirting the latter.*

the impression that there are only two major lines on that hand. This formation is called a simian line (fig. VI.8) and is frequently found on the hands of people suffering from Down's syndrome. It also appears sometimes on the hands of completely healthy people, but it is rare and hardly ever found on both hands unless the person has had Down's syndrome. Therefore we shall study the simian line along with the other major lines as if it were a fourth one.

The life line

One of the most common, widespread beliefs is that the length of our life line (fig.VI.9) is a sign of how long we will live.

Consequently, if we have a short life line, we will have a short life, but a long life line means we will live to a very ripe old age. However, this is quite a mistaken and dangerous theory: if we were to believe it, then if our life line is cut off it would lead us to think that it must denote a fatal accident.

Many years ago, an experience that I had when I was reading a young man's hand taught me that the meaning of this line is always in relation to life and movement and never to the moment of death.

The problem was that the life line on his right hand was cut off and as I have always considered that the right hand is home to our creative impulse and possibilities for the future, I began to suspect that this was a terrible sign and that the young man had only a short time to live. Fortunately, I was cautious enough not to alarm him with my clumsy interpretation.

However, all this made me think that if my theory was right then his heart and head lines should also be cut off, because when someone dies these vital organs shut down. Possibly, what I thought predicted a dreadful event would turn out to signify an important change in his life, prompted by a change in profession or family circumstances. As a matter of fact, time proved that I was right in thinking this because two years later this man decided to give up the job he had held down for fourteen years and set up a car repair shop. A year later he closed down the workshop and joined the fire brigade where he has worked happily ever since.

This has convinced me that this line tells us about past and present events and possibly

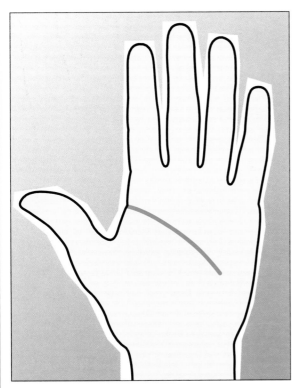

■ *Fig, VI.10. The head line starts together with the life line or just above it and crosses the palm towards the other edge.*

same way in the mind of a child as it is in the mind of an old person. So, how time is reflected in the hand will vary from one person to another and even from one part of the line to another on the same hand. We can attempt to fix the approximate date of an event only after properly studying the person's past and seeing how time develops on their hand. Even so we can make mistakes since, as we have said, a person's concept of time changes as they grow older.

In order to understand it better, imagine that this line is like a river with a strong current, rapids, eddies and still pools. We are sailing down the river and our only preoccupation is to keep our boat afloat and prevent it from capsizing. Everything that happens to us on our way is conveyed to our head line and our heart line, where we analyze the experience and create the necessary defence mechanisms. Therefore, when we come upon a whirlpool or a rapid further on we will know how to avoid them. Of course, the river will have tributaries and at times it will meander. In some stretches it may even disappear, show up again further on. The river's features will appear on our hands as crosses, squares, triangles and other symbols which we will look at in the next chapter.

Our life line brings us *joie de vivre,* the eager desire for adventure and also the courage that we need to enjoy the unique experience of life. It offers us the chance to decide what we want to do the following day, as long as we go with our life's current, and not against it. Its interior represents our feminine part, passive and maternal, and it is read in the direction of Venus and the thumb. Its exterior represents

about the future. It also warns us about illnesses and accidents but we cannot determine our exact moment of death from it.

The life line begins in the space between the thumb and index finger and skirts around the Mount of Venus. Many authors measure time on this line and even use number systems to work out the date on which a particular event took place. Nevertheless, we should accept that time is relative, even though we are used to measuring it with clocks, and that one minute can take up more or less space in our memories, depending on the intensity of the experience we lived through in that minute. And above all, time is not measured in the

the father figure, our active, masculine part, and it is read in the direction of Jupiter, the plain of Mars and the head and heart lines. In this way, we can see the balance between our male and female sides, how we attack and defend ourselves, or how we have assimilated our mother and father figures.

The head line

It too begins between the index finger and thumb, either above the life line or as part of it to begin with. It crosses the palm and ends either on the plain of Mars, on the Mount of Mars or on the Mount of the Moon. In some cases, as we have already mentioned, it joins up with the heart line to form the Simian line. It represents our intellectual development and faithfully judges the events shown on our life line (fig. VI.10).

The head line brings harmony to our hands, separating our ancient and modern heritage, and channelling our energy from reality to imagination. Throughout our lives it processes events, gathering necessary experiences. At the same time, it gives focus to our imagination. Its location on the plain of Mars means that it is continually in motion and it is the line which best reflects the present.

This is precisely its greatest strength; each change that we register in our mind, or whenever we discover the result of a problem, the codes of our magnificent computer-like mind process and transform our memories, our future projects and even our feelings, habits and tastes. One small thought can change the whole course of our lives.

If we observe this line we will see that it

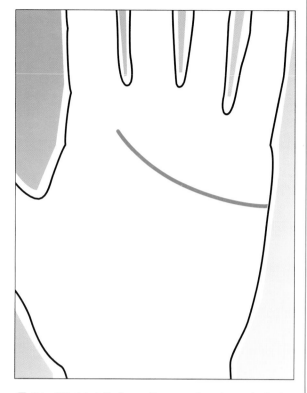

■ *Fig. VI.11. The heart line runs from beneath the little finger towards the middle or index finger.*

shows the most changes. Sometimes, it grows longer or varies in colour; in other cases, it grows faint or signs and shapes appear and disappear. There is constant activity on the head line just as there is in our minds, and it reflects to perfection our mental capacity now, as it was and as it can be in the future. Remember the general guidelines that we gave before: if the line is long it denotes intelligence and interest in intellectual matters, if it is short we limit our mental processes to matters of particular interest to us. The clarity or faintness of the line indicates our ability to concentrate. The straighter it is, the more practical and realistic the person will be. The more it curves the more indecisive they will be.

I do not like to talk about ill-fated markings on the hands since I do not believe in good without bad nor in positive without negative. There is a particular kind of head line which can be found on the hands of weak people with very flexible fingers. It is a faint and ragged line which ends in a star near the Mount of the Moon.

This line usually develops on the hands of very sensitive people who can sense and analyze situations which others cannot detect. They can show genius in any sphere that interests them. But this mental flexibility leads to such emotional sensitivity that if they are not lucky enough to find people who love and protect them their personalities can be destroyed and they could even suffer from an incurable mental illness.

The heart line

The heart line begins on the edge of the palm beneath the Mount of Mercury. It runs parallel to the head line and ends below the middle or index fingers (fig. VI.11). This line reveals our emotions, our degree of sensitivity and our ability to love. It is also a very good indication of the state of health of our heart. If before we said that the head line channels energy from the real world to our imagination, then the heart line does just the opposite, taking energy from our imagination to the real world. In other words, we need to be able to bring our imaginings into real life in order to find harmony (if our line ends in Saturn) or in order to discover and strengthen our personality (if it ends in Jupiter).

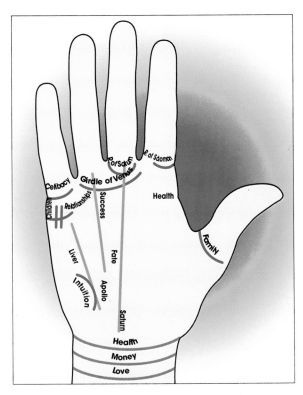

■ Fig. VI.12. Detail of the hand showing the minor lines and their most frequent paths.

Because of its location, this line receives all the energy of the palm and sends it out through the fingers. So we could say that we confront the world with feelings which have been judged by the head line and recorded by the life line. In the same way, the ideas that we receive come through the fingers, meeting first the heart line, then the head line and finally transforming our life line if the idea interests us.

However, the least important external events or feelings are reflected in the part of the line that faces the wrist; and our greatest loves and deepest feelings in the part facing the fingers. The line should be a good colour and there should be no chains and islands in its path.

It should arch slightly and preferrably it should end between Jupiter and Saturn, since this denotes harmony between our mind and our feelings.

People who have suffered many sentimental blows very often have areas of hardened skin on their hands, mainly in the area above the heart line and below the fingers. This line needs the backing of courage from the life line and intelligence from the head line in order to face the tasks listed in the chapter on the phalanxes of the fingers.

The Simian line

We have previously explained that this line is formed by the head and heart lines joined together. Another name that it is known by is the "line of concentrated power" because the powers of the two lines are united and concentrated in a single line (see fig. VI.8). It may appear as the result of a handicap, such as Down's syndrome, or the result of a dramatic incident which has changed our outlook on life. It can also be caused by persistent thought patterns.

To date I have not had the chance to examine the hands of anybody with Down's syndrome, but I have been able to analyze photocopies of the hands of three children between the ages of 7 and 10 who suffer from it. What surprised me most was to find film and cartoon characters represented on their hands, almost as if they were real people. This would seem to bear out the theory that these children live out fantasies more vividly than other children of their age.

Moreover, and judging by what their teachers had to say, these children do great justice to their simian line by lavishing out love and affection on anyone and everyone around them, and in particular on the people who look after them.

In the remaining cases, people who have a simian line on their hands usually devote all their energy to a single interest at a time. They love with great intensity and, at the same time, their partners must share their interests with equal devotion. If the hand is coarse it can sometimes indicate a violent and unpredictable nature.

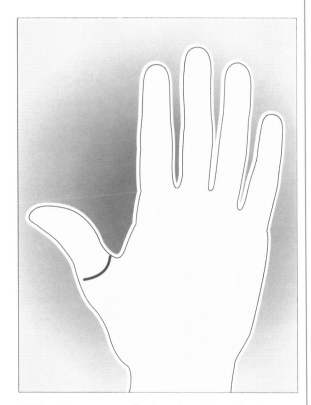

■ Fig. VI.13. Family line describing the kind of family the bearer has, its importance to him and his relationship with other members.

They live their feelings to the full, without thinking about what they are doing, even if they are clearly quick-witted and highly intelligent. If they become stubborn, or if they are wilful and capricious it is advisable to help them find an ideal in which to channel their energies.

MINOR LINES

The results of recent research into human embryos shows that the lines of the hand develop very early on. Sometimes they even develop before movement is detected. In the eighth week, the life line begins to appear, followed by the heart line and finally the head line. Then other lines, whcih are known as minor lines, begin to develop; in many cases they are present on the hands of new-born babies but sometimes they emerge later (fig. VI.12).

Some people would seem to be destined from birth to undergo a certain experience or learn a particular lesson and, try though they might to avoid it, it will hound them until they face it.

More often than not, a minor line is a sign that we must deal with these outstanding matters. The path of the line will also indicate that if we successfully complete these tasks, which perhaps were assigned to us before we were born, we will feel freer and less burdened.

The danger of these minor lines lies in the fact that many authors are totally convinced that they have discovered a line whose meaning throws a new light on the reading of hands. If we were to allow this tendency to get out of control, then chirology might be turned

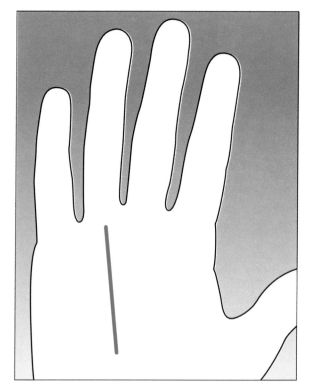

Fig. VI.14. A clear success line indicates the owner's success and how he is looked on by society.

into a treatise on statistics, or even into a new computer programme. In an endeavour to avoid this, I will set out the most common and reliable lines: the family line, the success line, the lines of relationships and children, the fate line, Venus's girdle, the rings of Saturn and Solomon, and the bracelets.

If someone does not have any, or only some of these minor lines, it is not a bad sign. Quite the contrary, a hand with few lines always reminds me of a blank page waiting to be filled in by its owner. Furthermore, people who have very few lines will have fewer nerve endings in their hand. Therefore they will be better at putting up with physical pain and enduring hardship without complaining. As a

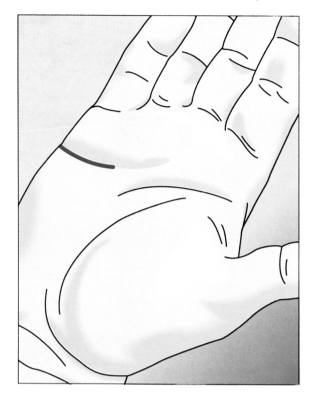

■ *Fig. VI.15. One or more lines describe relations with our partner and our commitment to them.*

Our concept of the family will depend on whether we have a single line, or two parallel lines. Some people distinguish between their paternal family and the family that they form through marriage; these people will have two lines. For other people, all their relatives form a single family, so they have a single line.

The second family line reflects our ideal, and so it determines the kind of family unit we will strive for with our partner. These lines appear as rings on the phalanx of the thumb closest to the palm, and the further up the thumb the rings are, the less realistic we are.

The success line

When it begins beneath the Mount of Apollo it indicates our chances of success in life. It is a vertical line which can be long or short. Some chirologists call it the line of capacity, since its presence indicates a capacity for great achievement in life. The line must be strong, clear and straight; any deviation could indicate that we may be forced to make difficult concessions on the road to success.

If the line is interrupted we too will suffer interruptions before finding the profession to which we are best suited.

If the line is crossed by others, success will be a long time in coming and if it does come it may be late in life.

Occasionally, there are two parallel lines; this could indicate that success is indirect and linked to our partner's success in which we may have played a part (fig. VI.14).

result, they will be far better at concentrating their time and energy on the truly important things in life.

In short, what we must aim to do is to interpret all the lines that we do see, but not despair if they are not present.

Family line

This line or lines are located in the phalanx of the thumb nearest the palm. The first lines that form, at the base of the thumb, portray our view of family life. They usually take the form of chains which represent the emotional or psychological ties between us and each family member (fig. VI.13).

Relationship lines

All chirologists agree that these are small horizontal lines located on the Mount of Mercury. They begin at the edge of the hand and run towards the heart line. They denote love affairs that have made a deep impression on us.

However, when we have a steady relationship, one of these short lines may confront another vertical one which starts at the heart line and runs across the hand towards the life line. This is considered by many authors to be the hepatic line or health line which analyzes our physical constitution. To me, it describes the relationship we have with our partner.

The decision to share our life with someone is of the utmost importance and its mark on our hands could not be limited to those small lines on the Mount of Mercury.

It deserves a line of its own in contact with the three major lines. It is also logical that this line should not be joined to the other small horizontal ones since not all the important relationships in our lives end in cohabitation.

It is often the case that a relationship with one person can go through so many different stages that it feels as though we have lived with several different people.

Therefore if we want to analyze someone's true relationship, and not their imaginary ones, we must begin by looking at the short horizontal line which starts at the edge of the hand and clearly confronts the other vertical line running from the heart line to the fate line or the life line (fig. VI.15).

Children lines

These are small, parallel, vertical lines located over one of the relationship lines on the Mount of Mercury. They are usually clearer on women's hands than on men's and they represent our potential children, since abortions and miscarriages are also recorded.

I have even seen these lines fade when clients have been predicted more children than they wanted and have subsequently chosen a reliable method of contraception.

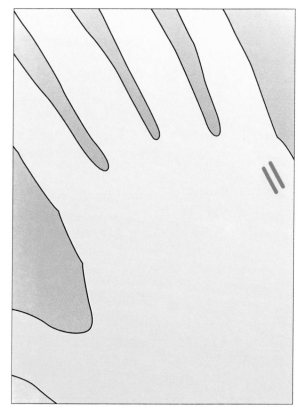

■ *Fig. VI.16. Lines showing the number of children we may have.*

Adoptions are also recorded on the hands long before the decision to adopt is reached. These lines are separate from the relationship lines.

When a woman is pregnant, one of the lines representing children becomes a brighter or stronger colour and sometimes turns a shiny white. At the same time, a small cross appears on the life line and a brilliant circle forms on the Mount of Venus where it joins the Mount of Mars. The part of the circle facing the wrist is fringed with purple.

■ *Fig. VI.17. The fate line describes developments in our career.*

The lines representing children can be long or short. The former denotes a child with a strong character while the latter indicates a more sensitive nature. That is why long lines have traditionally been thought to represent boys, and short lines girls (fig. VI.16).

Fate line

Although it figures as a minor line, the fate line is an important component of our reading. Basically, it describes our career but its location on the hand makes it a valuable channel of energy since it divides the palm in two, running from the valley of Neptune to the Mount of Saturn (fig. VI.17). Some authors call it the Karma line because it shows the choices fate offers us. When it deviates from its usual route and fades into the life line it indicates that our job or occupation is a burden to us and that our destiny lies in a different direction.

Its path through the valley of Neptune tells us about the present. The lines which intersect it or strengthen it represent people who help or hinder us.

Lines from the Mount of the Moon which end near the fate line or join it denote new ideas in our work or plans for starting up a business. In many cases, the relationship lines cross the fate line revealing the possibility of disagreements with our partner for devoting too much time to our career and forgetting about our family obligations.

A line within the life line but running parallel to the fate line indicates that we have found the job for which we are best fitted and are on the right track in life.

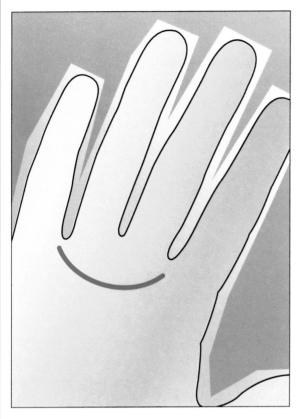

■ *Fig. VI.18. Girdle of Venus, capacity for seduction.*

In fact, those with this mark are passionate, energetic and given to excessive flights of imagination and drama. That is why some chirologists consider it to be an ill-fated line which predicts vices, defects and, above all, infidelity. But what it really indicates is that its bearers will have their own moral code, together with a strong sensuality which may shock more conservative or methodical minds.

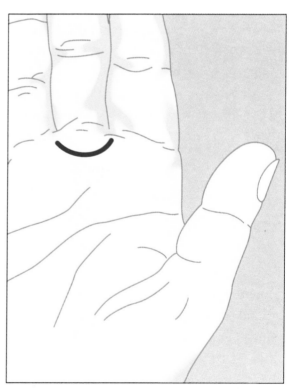

■ *Fig. VI.19. Ring of Saturn. capacity for intellectual comprehension.*

The Girdle of Venus

This line starts within the heart line and skirts the Mounts of Apollo and Saturn. Those few people who have it possess charm and a special power of seduction that nobody is impervious to. Joy, an altruistic nature and intense sexuality are the gifts of Venus to these people but, like her, they tend to be drawn into stormy relationships, although they are victorious in the end (fig. VI.18).

If the girdle is broken or made up of small lines its meaning is weakened, leading to a continual feeling of dissatisfaction with decisions based on intuition.

When the girdle opens up so that it seems to start off within one of the relationship lines its bearer will worship their partner, giving them all their affection and doing everything in their power to make the relationship last.

several, even though they are unfinished, it means that we have studied different philosophies and gained greater insight into man's psychological makeup.

In those rare cases when this line is perfectly formed we will have before us a person of great wisdom, in control of his own mind and able to understand other people's. He will help others disinterestedly. He is an initiate (fig. VI.20).

Ring of Saturn

This ring surrounds the middle finger on the Mount of Saturn, even though it is very rarely found. It intensifies the powers of the Mount after which it is named and points to a great possibility of intellectual success. Nevertheless, this talent for understanding everything at a theoretical level can lead to great instability when it comes to solving problems in real life, and people who have this ring are very often lonely, melancholy people (fig. VI.19).

Ring of Solomon

This ring surrounds the index finger on the Mount of Jupiter. It rarely forms a perfect ring around the finger but we often find small arcs which begin over the life line and end in the middle of the Mount. Up to two or three of these partial rings are present on many hands. They tell us about our wisdom and philosophical capacity. Therefore, when there are

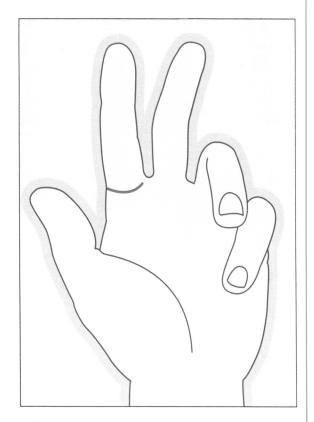

■ *Fig. VI.20. The Ring of Solomon denotes a good philosophy of life.*

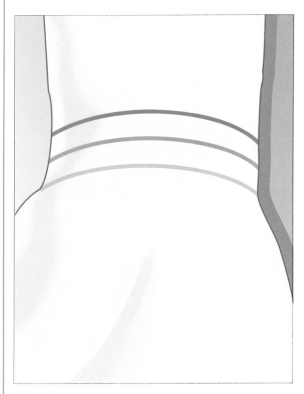

■ *Fig. VI.21. Bracelets summarizing the three pillars of mankind: health, wealth and love.*

Bracelets

These three lines surround our wrists like bracelets. On some hands it looks as though the-

re are only two because the third one is very faint or broken up (fig. VI. 21).

Our hands provide such a complete reading that we could not do without these few lines to summarize the great book of life. People are usually interested in three main areas of life: health, money and love. The bracelets deal with precisely these topics.

They are read from beneath the thumb of the left hand across both wrists to the thumb of the right hand. The nearest to the palm reveals our physical development and possible illnesses. The second one shows our economic possibilities and the last one how we love and are loved.

In the next chapter we will analyze symbols. These complement the meaning of the lines and make for a more accurate and pleasant reading. They throw more light on events registered by our lines and make their meaning clearer. However, I cannot stress how important it is always to give a complete reading of both hands, even though we work with one small area at a time. If we do not observe both hands and take into account the psychological makeup they reveal to us, then we may make mistakes and mislead our client.

CHAPTER VII

SIGNS AND SYMBOLS

Since the dawn of mankind we have striven to understand the environment in which we live, investing such simple drawings as signs and symbols with the power to represent a multitude of ideas and emotions. Sometimes the meaning of these drawings is so abstract that it would be very difficult to explain, and even more difficult to understand. Some of these signs and symbols form part of our collective unconscious; they are understood and used by all men, regardless of differences in language, culture, religion or politics. Even though we may not know their meaning, their mere presence causes violent stirrings in the depths of our subconscious, awakening strong feelings of rejection or acceptance which are capable of upsetting us and changing our mood.

These symbols have been used by all civilizations. Throughout history. In magic and in various religions they are seen as keys which unlock communications between the sky and the earth, and control the forces of nature with their presence.

In wartime, victory has owed much to the colours and emblems on a flag; the mere sight of a cross has halted invading armies and the red cross has been respected in the very heart of the battle. On the other hand, when men have decided to defy symbols by destroying, burning or trampling them underfoot, a curse would seem to befall them and punish them for such an affront.

There is something quite fascinating and magnetic about symbols which means that, although everyone may react differently to them, no one is completely indifferent to them. The evocative wisdom enclosed in their

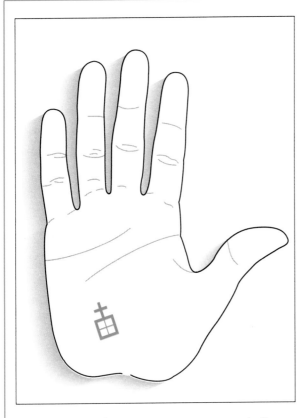

advanced than ours which were probably destroyed by natural disasters on a gigantic scale. They claim that symbols are all that are left of these cultures.

Be that as it may, what is really important is the image that symbols conjure up in our minds and the use to which we put them today, especially since many of these signs and symbols are printed on our hands. It is with just such freshness that our minds convey their most incorruptible thoughts to us. Let us go on to analyze the most frequent signs, which because of their simplicity have the clearest meanings.

THE CROSS

The cross is man's most ancient symbol. It is formed by two lines; the vertical line which represents the spirit and the horizontal line which represents matter.

Man alone in all Nature has been chosen to be a magician, transforming the power from above so that it can be seen here on Earth. Only he can make the sign of the cross with his body; he need only lift his arms at right angles.

In arithmetic, the cross is the addition sign and when turned a little, the multiplication sign. This is precisely its meaning, for if we add up our experiences one after another our life is enriched and our capabilities multiply. That is why we could say that the cross is a sacrifice or a test that we choose to undergo to help others or to help ourselves. In effect, it is a circumstance which interrupts our chosen path in life.

meaning is still the best means of communication we have today.

It remains a quite mystery just who created these signs and symbols; the most we can hope to determine is when they were adopted by a certain community but, as soon as we feel sure about this, the symbols confound us by appearing in connection to the remains of an even older civilization.

Some theories claim that they are the legacy of beings from other planets who visited Earth in the infancy of mankind. Others claim that divine beings aided early man in his development and instilled in him veneration and respect for these signs. Some people prefer to believe in lost civilizations far more

Many people see the cross as an ill-fated sign, since we all know in our subconscious that when it appears we will have to forgo or exchange something if we want to proceed. It can be interpreted as an exam, part of a small assessment of a certain event, or as a partial or total judgement on our life so far.

Besides, if we stop to consider the places where we see this sign in our society (churches, places of healing, schools and cemeteries), we will see that they are all places where we stop to try to improve our education, our morals or our health, and, in the case of the cemetery, where our bodies find eternal rest. For this reason, whenever a cross appears on our hand, in or above a square, it signifies one of these places (fig. VII.1).

Nevertheless, if before we said that a line is like a canal that carries energy from one point of the hand to another, if two lines cross we will also have a crossing of energies, two forces confronting each other. If a cross appears on the mount of Jupiter, near the life line, it represents two people united in search of harmony. It symbolizes the perfect union and shows that we have found or are going to find our perfect partner, the person who will give us the chance to understand ourselves as we really are. In short, the key to self-understanding. Some chirologists refer to this cross as the happy marriage cross (fig. VII.2).

As we have seen, although the cross has many meanings, its interpretation is simple and specific.

The best way to read this symbol is to imagine that we are following a path and that the appearance of a cross represents a fork or a crossroads. We must stop and decide which road to take: do we go straight on or turn off to one side? Our hand is wise and it will show us which arm of the cross is whiter or redder, longer or shorter, which one is straighter and clearer, or points to a particular place. All this will help us to decide whether we stop and take time to choose or whether we take whatever path we fancy without a thought for the consequences.

Generally speaking, if the cross appears in the vicinity of the valley of Neptune, the crossroads will refer to our studies or work (fig. VII.3). It indicates that something is wrong in our professional life; we are not put-

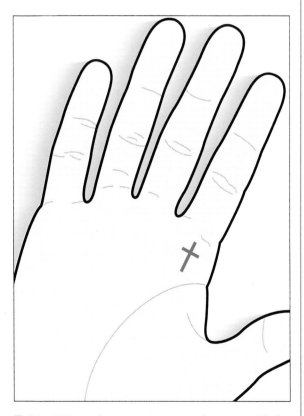

■ *Fig. VII.2. A cross on Jupiter indicates a well-chosen partner. It is called the happy marriage cross.*

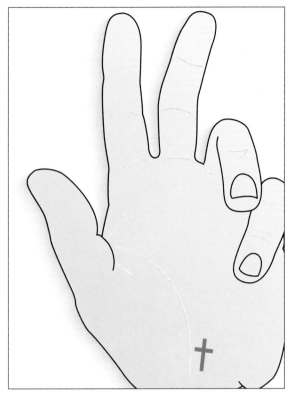

■ *Fig. VII.3. A cross in the valley of Neptune can indicate exams or interruptions in our professional life.*

not necessarily be the protagonist. For example, our boss's retirement will be marked by a cross near our fate line, since it can benefit or harm us. Even though we cannot control this event, what we can do is to endeavour to turn it to our advantage.

However, we should not look upon the cross as a punishment. Quite the contrary, we should cherish this humble sign which allows us to change our fanatical and conservative attitudes and analyze each circumstance from a different point of view. If we look a little, the cross could be the skeleton or start of other shapes, such as the triangle or the square, which we will study later. Therefore, the acceptance of the cross is not a moral or religious question. It is important to grasp its

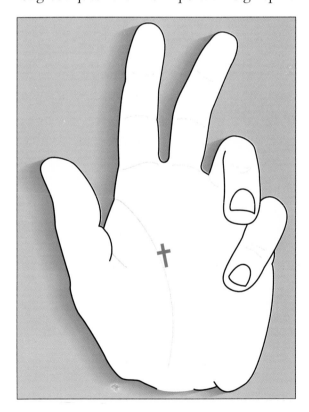

■ *Fig. VII.4. A cross on the life line indicates that something will interrupt our daily life.*

ting enough energy into it because we do not know how to channel our energy properly. If it appears near the life line it will mean hold-ups, minor accidents, illness or even pregnancies and births; anything which interrupts our daily life (fig. VII.4). If it appears on or near the heart line it means interruptions in our feelings or conflicts which will oblige us to take new roads (fig.VII.5). On the head line it shows a new way of looking at things (fig. VII.6).

It is important to remember always that our hands reflect both our interior and our exterior at the same time; although everything they show us will affect our lives, we will

meaning, since although it denotes conflicts, sacrifices or annoying interruptions; it also forces us to bring our body and spirit into harmony.

As a general rule the whole hand must be analyzed; one symbol contributes information but can never be the key to someone's life. We must add up and summarize all the information and not tell half truths. Only then can we come close to visualizing the jigsaw of man's complex life.

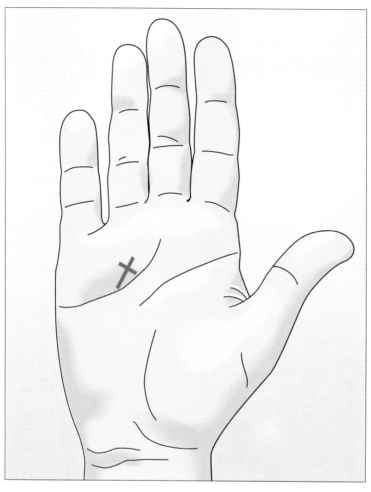

■ *Fig. VII.5 A cross on the heart line warns us of love conflicts.*

stead of against him. In this way he observed that cold and heat, along with the sun's rays, come from different directions, so that if he built a square dwelling he could make best use of the heat and the daylight, and find shelter at the hottest time of day

Before, the weather was his worst enemy and forced him to take shelter below ground but, with the aid of the square, it became his ally and he could conserve its energy for when he needed it.

THE SQUARE

The square probably made its appearance in man's history when he first decided to leave his cave and build a dwelling to protect him from predators and from the weather.

In order to build this place of refuge and rest, he discovered that he could join forces with nature and make it work for him in-

Man discovered that with this type of dwelling he could spot his enemies before they attacked, so he could be ready to fight or run away if necessary.

This shape also allowed him to position entrances and exits for his convenience and safety, and to enjoy greater freedom than he had in the caves. Apart from providing shelter from the weather and a warm dwelling, the square was found to be a practical, adaptable shape. For that reason man began to use it regularly for the useful things he invented, as well as in the blocks of adobe and stone, and in the bricks and tiles that he used for his buildings.

As soon as he had created a safer place to live, man experienced a sense of ownership. He began to think about the future now that he was able to store food and objects which

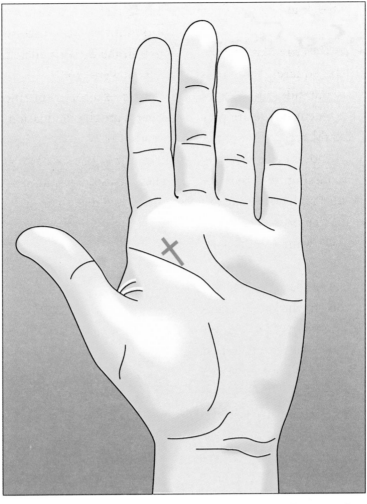

■ *Fig. VII.6. A cross on the head line will force us to change our line of thought.*

Safety and convenience gradually hemmed him in, and later forced him into new patterns of behaviour. Now he had to plan ahead, make laws about his acts and about his property, and ultimately set up a stable community. This was to would lead the way to subsequent civilizations.

If one bears in mind the usefulness of the square, man has used it for keeping and protecting

before he had to carry with him, and he was no longer limited in size and number.

Now he found it easier to store things up in times of plenty for use in times of shortage. He managed to overcome deep fears and anxieties but, at the same time, he found himself tied to his house. It was no longer a simple matter to move to a more advantageous place, without leaving behind everything he had stored up.

things of value to him. Not only does he use it in his buildings and in his streets and highways, but also to preserve his culture in manuscripts, documents and books. He uses just such a shape for his furniture and vehicles, to build stairs, frame his works of art and safeguard his money and valuables.

This need for property and protection associated with the square is so deeply rooted in us that it is unconsciously reflected in our hands. It encloses a setback and protects us from it.

If before we said that the cross was like sitting an exam, then the square is our pass mark. In it we see the four sides of an experience and from that moment on we are protected from it if it should recur. But sometimes the square on our hands is not completely formed. If one side is missing, we have not quite passed the exam although we are close to it. We have yet to master one of the four areas of assessment if we want to complete the square.

One very good example that comes to my mind is the case of a woman who came to consult me about certain problems that she was having in her marriage. She had been married for eight years and unable to have children. Consequently, she had devoted herself to her husband, playing the role of wife, lover, friend and mother all in one.

She had decided to turn a blind eye to his occasional love affairs, believing that it was for the good of her marriage, especially since her husband never stopped showing that he loved and needed her. However, she came to see me because she had begun to suspect that one woman had become special to her husband and that she could not bear. She had decided to leave him, despite his attempts to make her change her mind.

When I looked closely at her hands, I noticed a half-finished square on her relationship line. The line nearest to the mount of Jupiter was missing, indicating that, even though she had done her utmost to protect her marriage and had fought against every threat, she was not able to ward off the humi-

liating idea that another woman could be as important to her husband as she was, even though she was not, in fact, sure that her suspicions were true.

This example confirmed the theory that squares are the foundation of everything that we want to construct, the stairs or ladder that help us to rise to higher levels of knowledge. They are the paving stones which we lay down in order to make our path through life easier to follow.

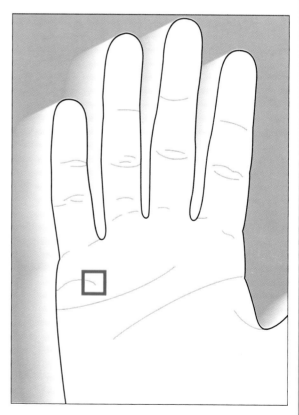

■ *Fig. VII.7. The square is the symbol of protection. In this drawing it is protecting the relationship line.*

The square is a common sign on our hands because we all have something to protect ourselves against or some experience we wish to remember and learn from.

Therefore when we interpret a square, we must take into consideration the position of any important lines that are close to it; whether it is fully or only partially formed, and its colour, as well as any details inside it.

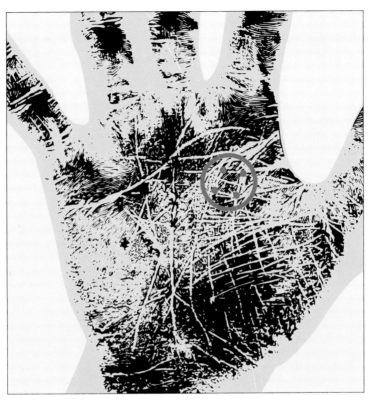

■ *Fig. VII.8. Square-shaped palm print full of signs, triangles, stars, etc.*

THE TRIANGLE

If we draw a straight line and join the two arms of a cross we get a triangle, and if we draw a diagonal line from one corner of a square to another we get two. This shape represents a test, or more precisely, what we have learnt from that test. It symbolizes the creative origin of nature, something which is born, develops, grows and bears fruit. It is also a sign of power in the zodiac because it can unite three signs of the same element.

It is found in the symbolic alphabets in use prior to the captivity of Babylon and in magic ciphers, such as those used in alchemy, as well as in others attributed to the Templars. It is frequently drawn on pentacles, talismans and amulets, and plays a major role in mathematics and numbers. It was the right-angled triangle that lead Pythagoras to create his world famous theorem, which is now the cornerstone of the philosophy of numbers.

According to the followers of the occult, the number three, represented by the triangle, was a sign of "the idea" which could be multiplied ad infinitum, whether on the physical, moral or intellectual plane. For that reason they made a clear distinction between active, passive and neutral. In their own words:

what's above is below
sufficing their fusion
to bring about the miracle
since everything was,
is and will be
absolute in the absolute

The number six, or two triangles, signified the balance between ideas or between the microcosmos and the macrocosmos. The number nine, or three triangles, denoted the perfection of ideas.

In the Hindu religion the trinity is formed by Brahma, Vishnu and Shiva. The Brahmin have three great Vedas, three Margas or roads to salvation, three jewels of wisdom. Shiva is represented with three eyes on her forehead.

For the Ancient Greeks the number three was the origin of all known things. So they made their predictions over a tripod and drank three times in honour of the three Graces. Three gods ruled the world: Jupiter, Neptune and Pluto. Three knocks opened a door and three signals marked the start of a race or a game.

The Egyptians built their pyramids on a square base with triangular outer walls to symbolize the creative origin of Nature; and many a historian believes that secret initiation rites were held inside.

The triangle is the bridge leading to our spirit, the vat from which we extract the essence of ideas. This shape appears when we have isolated the positive part of an experience and risen a little above material matters. "When a pupil is ready a teacher appears." This sums up the triangle which appears when our mind is ready for improvement and opportunities present themselves.

On the life line it means that we have learnt from our experiences, and on the heart line that we are more aware of the importance of our feelings. On the head line it shows psychic development. Even though the trian-

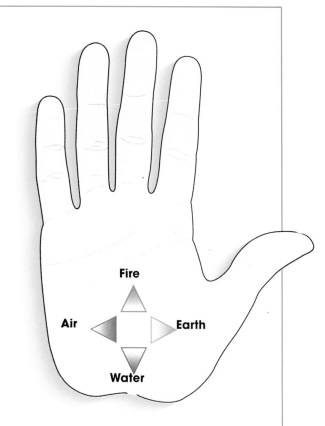

■ *Fig. VII.9. Position of the triangles on the hands. Each one points to a different element.*

gle joins three of the four elements with all its might, the vertex will usually point to the dominant one. This, and its position on the hand, makes a triangle easier to interpret. Therefore, four triangles are possible (fig. VII.9); when one appears on our fate line it represents a course of study which will further our career (fig. VII. 10.).

Fire Triangle

Its vertex points upwards towards the fingers and it denotes moral capacity and strength.

97

Water Triangle

Its vertex points down towards the wrist and its power is to seduce and conquer whoever or whatever we desire.

Air Triangle

When the vertex points towards the creativity curve it denotes intellectual powers.

Earth Triangle

The vertex pointing towards the thumb means power over material things: a lucky win, an unexpected inheritance, a prize etc., especially if the inside of the triangle is a shiny white.

Here is an anecdote to end the explanation of the triangle. Five years ago I was invited to give a talk about the occult in a discotheque in Madrid to celebrate Midsummer Night. The idea appealed to me: chirology has always had a rather sinister reputation but I was being given the chance to pass on its message in a place solely for entertainment and, above all, to young people. The experience promised to be interesting and I took up the challenge.

■ *Fig. VII.10. Detail of triangle on the fate line.*

Since the talk was to be broadcast on the radio for the benefit of those who could not attend in person, the participants were seated with the radio presenter at a long table on the stage. The discotheque was packed out and everyone was out to enjoy themselves. I let myself be swept along on the wave of euphoria and when my turn came to explain about the art of hand-reading, I let the radio presenter persuade me to give a live reading for the first time in my life, and against my principles since I have always taken my work very seriously.

However, I made it quite clear that this demonstration had nothing to do with a complete reading of hands; I would say a little about personality and the most obvious signs on the hand. The presenter suggested I read the hands of the first five people to come up. There was a general rush and I suddenly found a very attractive woman in front of me, hand outstretched, waiting to have it read. All I remember seeing was a triangle which was forming next to the fate line with its vertex pointing towards the mount of the Moon. I predicted that she was about to begin some studies that would change her outlook on life and, consequently, her destiny.

Months later, I agreed to give a course on chirology at a holistic centre and amongst the students was that same young lady. Today she is one of my best friends and an accomplished chirologist whom I like to boast about whenever I can. The triangle on her hand was proved right.

THE STAR

Ever since time immemorial, Man has gazed at the night sky and the shining stars have filled him with hope. However gloomy a road may seem to be there is always a star to guide us on our way.

Even if our loved ones are many thousands of miles away, the stars are our common point of reference and it comforts us to think that they too could be looking up at them. When we look at the stars, we become aware that, just like us, people all around the world may be contemplating the same spectacular night sky with feelings of happiness or in moments of suffering.

A man can lose everything at the drop of a hat, but every night the stars will come out like Nature's special gift to us.

Man has always longed to reach out and touch the stars. In the belief that the first people to set foot on them would rule the world, we have developed our civilizations and our technology to that end. But we have had to

come a long way to get where we are now. It all began with the first wizards who saw the Universe as a gigantic spider's web whose invisible threads linked stars, animals, plants, objects, insects, humans and all existing matter in such a way that any movement or change on the part of any one of these things affected the whole Universe. So it was that the movement of a star affected man just as man's actions affected the star and one of the most ancient occult sciences known to man was born: astrology.

Later, in 1543, Nicholas Copernicus discovered that the Earth was not the centre of the

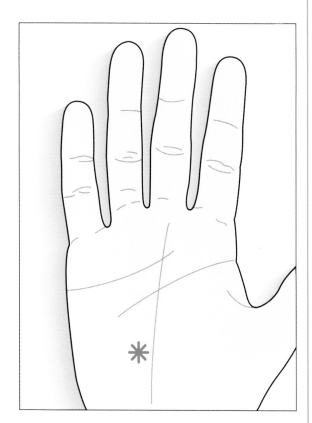

■ *Fig. VII.11. A star near the fate line indicates a work-related association.*

Universe but that it revolved around the Sun. In 1632, with the aid of a telescope, Galileo confirmed Copernicus' ideas. This was the beginning of a new science of the stars called astronomy, which fast grew away from its parent. Meanwhile, with the discovery of new planets, the foundations of the old school of astrology began to crack and had to be revised to keep up with the new times.

Today, even though we have set foot on the Moon, we are beginning to think that perhaps our ancestors' theories about alchemy, astrology, medicine and chirology were not so far from the truth and that if we applied our present knowledge to their work, man could perhaps discover the secret of his existence.

The symbol of the star is so deeply rooted in us that the expert in perception psychology, Karl Zener, included it, along with the cross, the square, the circle and wavy lines, in his famous Zener Cards. He designed the pack for carrying out experiments into extrasensory perception, and his cards are still used today. The results have aroused a lively interest among intellectuals, psychologists, psychiatrists and the governments of many countries. In his day, the eminent Swiss psychiatrist Carl Jung was very taken with their results.

In tarot, card number XVII is the Star. This card is interpreted by tarot readers as representing hope, truth and love. However, a star also appears as the Empress' crown on card number III, while on card number XV, the Devil, it takes the form of an inverted pentacle, a five-pointed star.

Its meaning is widespread in folklore and we often refer to the stars when we speak about good or bad fortune. It also denotes a famous person whose talent shines out.

If before we said that the cross represented the meeting of two forces, then the star represents the union of several forces. If the former stood for an experience under assessment, then the latter stands for an exam on all the subjects at once. A cross formed by straight lines inter-

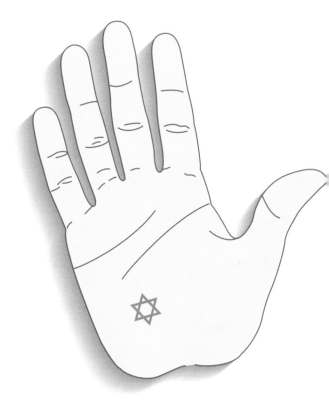

■ *Fig. VII.12. The Star of David, or six-pointed star, symbol of the Jewish people. The twelve angles represent the twelve tribes of Israel.*

secting in the middle shows courage and daring to confront several forces or personalities at once. Our economic, moral or mental development will gain in strength if we are able to handle this situation. On the other hand, if we act rashly and do not know how to confront these forces we risk being engulfed by them.

The star may remind us of the spokes in a wheel. Once in motion it starts to go faster and faster, speeding up our experiences and our development. However, we must always drive at the right speed, otherwise we run the risk of losing control and crashing.

If a star is located near our fate line, it suggests that a business is about to be set up (fig. VII.11). It is very important to look at the colour of and analyze the lines, as each one represents a partner. The further from the fate line, the more likely it is to be a sign of intellectual or philanthropic pursuits. A star at the start of the life line will give us the power to neutralize dangerous situations both for our-

selves and all those who are with us. It is the advantage of being born with good fortune, or a lucky star.

The star of David, two equilateral triangles forming a six-pointed star, is recognised worldwide as the symbol of the Jewish people. Its origin is unknown and presumably not Jewish since it was adopted by them at the time of their captivity and exile in Babylon in the year 6 B.C. In Jewish lore, the six points represent the six days of creation as well as North, South, East, West, up and down. The twelve angles symbolize the twelve tribes of Israel, whilst its symmetry reflects the balance between the material and the spiritual world (fig. VII.12).

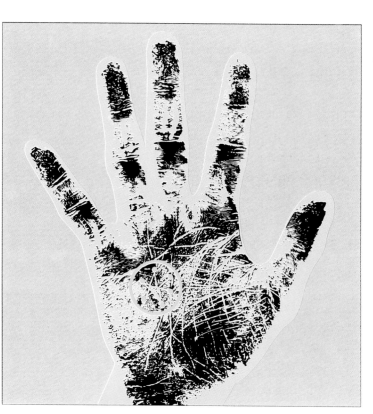

■ *Fig. VII.13. A star near the head line may indicate a very intelligent person who knows how to get out of very difficult situations*

It has been said that the Jews are an ancient people who, in their time, had not attained a high enough degree of evolution to pass on to a superior plane of consciousness. For that reason, they are condemned to relive their experiences until they can at last reach their promised land. In the meantime they will continue to wander, persecuted by others, despite the Bible's claim that they were chosen by God to safeguard his Word and its mysteries. According to this idea, the triangle which forms part of the star of David and which points downwards shows their need to go down into hell to purify their souls through suffering. The triangle which points upwards shows the opportunity to climb up to superior planes, once the necessary lessons have been learnt.

When a perfectly formed star can be seen (fig. VII.13) we have before us a person of great wisdom who feels the need to share his experiences with others, wandering endlessly from one place to another and undergoing difficult trials, although he will always have that rare ability to call up his positive energy and come through unscathed.

THE CIRCLE

Of all Nature's forces, the cyclone must surely be the most feared by man since, with its swirling motion, it sucks up and destroys everything in its path at such speed that escape is impossible. Nothing is safe, and there is no form of protection. Also, under still water, deadly whirlpools can lie in wait for the unwary. In dry, desert lands it is easy to lose your bearings and end up walking in circles until, exhausted, you die of thirst or are devoured by wild animals. Circular, too, are the craters or mouths of volcanoes which spew out smoke, ashes, lava and enough fiery matter to bury whole cities.

Generally speaking, man has always been forced to forge ahead into the future without

time to look back. The circle awakens fear in him since however much he advances he always comes back to the same place. Circles enclose and imprison, leaving no way out. Our collective subconscious usually associates them with dangerous, unnerving places and upsets. Circuses and amphitheatres are circular in shape, undoubtedly to let spectators get a better view but, nevertheless, some bloody spectacles have been staged within them.

■ *Fig. VII.14. The circle traps and encloses us, making us turn our thoughts over in our mind without looking for a solution.*

Nowadays, bullrings, a vestige of those Roman and Greek games, continue to encapsulate the meaning of the circle. A man confronts a wild animal in the ring and cannot leave it until one conquers, killing or injuring the other. This sums up the circle; something is caught inside it and must die or come to an end before life can continue. If the cross makes us think things over, the square protects us and our valuables and the triangle raises our intellectual and spiritual level, then the circle traps us and exhausts us in our efforts to escape. Our only chance is to confront bravely the experience and overcome it. Fortunately, a perfect circle is rarely found on the hand (fig. VII.14). We more often see semi-circles, half-moons, and curves which could be forming drawings of roads or cylindrical objects which point to particular events in our everyday lives and not to any unresolved problems or negative aspects of our character.

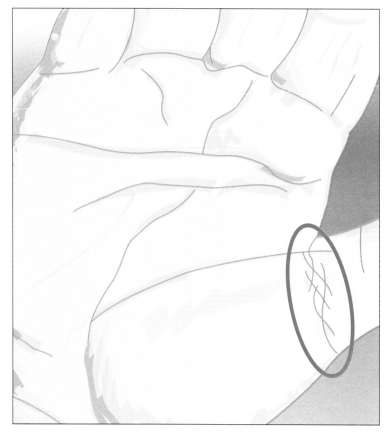

■ *Fig. VII.15. Sometimes we let the chains enslave us.*

On the other hand, we live on a spherical planet, and although it is true that only death can free us from its influence, it is no less true that it is the ideal place in which to learn how to make the most of life. Even though the circle would appear to be a negative symbol we should see it as just one more shape that teaches us to understand our fellow men and the world around us.

This is how our ancestors saw it when they overcame their fear and began to turn the circle to their advantage. They invented the wheel and its many variants, revolutionizing technology and making life so much easier. Thanks to the cylinder we can move huge weights, cover great distances in a short time, harness the energy of water and air, make pulleys, spin wool and other natural fibres, grind cereals and other foods and learn about mechanics, which has enabled us to create a multitude of machines from watches to cars.

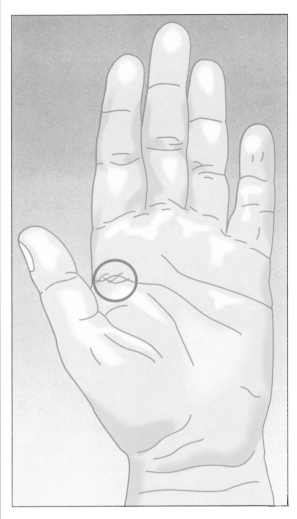

In magic, the circle or zero symbolizes all or nothing, 'the infinite', and provides complete protection during magic rites. No 'occult power' can violate the magic circle but neither can we receive help from outside it. Remember that today the circular traffic signs are those that forbid or oblige us to make certain manoeuvres, whilst at the same time they limit the time and place of the prohibition.

After all that has been said, we should be forewarned against being trapped in the vicious circles of our experiences. But if we ever do make that mistake we must banish any negative thoughts at once.

Other more benign and less powerful circular forms also appear quite frequently on our hands. We give them these names: chains, the island and the cigar.

As is to be expected, chains denote slavery. They form on the lines of our hands and their whereabouts indicate what area of our lives has become imprisoned, or what person or event has deprived us of our freedom (fig. VII. 15).

The island forms in the middle of a line and indicates an interruption (fig. VII.16). In order to understand this symbol we need only look at *Robinson Crusoe*, that incredible novel written by Daniel Defoe.

Crusoe decides to leave the safety and comfort of his home for the excitement of travel and new experiences. After several journeys, young Robinson is shipwrecked on the way to the African coasts. He is the only survivor who manages to reach the shore. He finds himself on an island and is faced with all the fears and anxieties that have threatened mankind since

Furthermore, since man learnt to make fire, people of all cultures have sat in circles to exchange ideas and reach agreements on their future. From King Arthur's famous Round Table and the forum of the Roman Senate to the present day, circles have gathered people together, whether to discuss politics, economics or science or for entertainment or altruistic ends.

the beginning of time. He has to overcome his limitations and relearn all the knowledge he inherited in his time. At first he did not realize that the real a d v e n t u r e would take place inside him.

However, he soon learns and once he has taken care of his basic needs, hunting, farming and putting the island's resources to good use, he begins to learn about himself and gradually develops his spirituality.

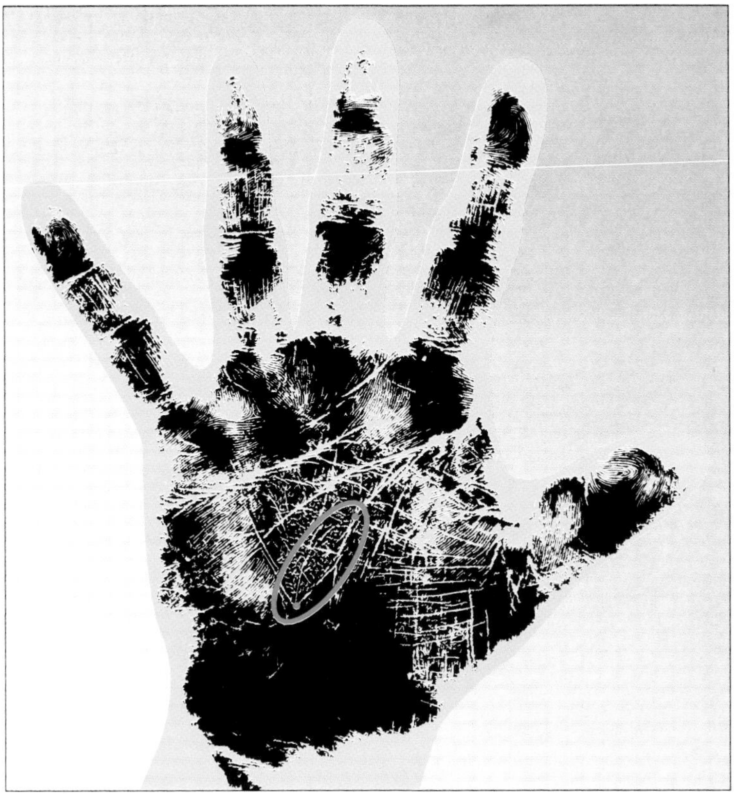

■ *Fig. VII.17. The cigar indicates that the person expresses himself in a different way.*

look inside ourselves and discover our true feelings, our hidden capacities or our most positive attitudes.

The cigar (fig. VII.17) is present on the hands of people who express themselves differently from those around them. They may speak a different language or dialect, or be able to communicate more extensively with others using their bodies or their minds.

His unselfishness, reflection of the island's generosity, leads him to bestow all his affection on a savage; a cannibal whom he calls Friday. He educates Friday and comes to look upon him as a son, taking him with him when he manages to escape from the island.

What this book teaches us is that there are times in our lives when we need to cut ourselves off from the outside world in order to

THE TRIDENT

Neptune carried a trident to symbolize his power over three forces of nature: water, storms and earthquakes. When this sign appears on our hands we know that we have a moral duty to comply with. We have been given energy and specific powers for that purpose and it would be wrong to waste them (fig. VII.18).

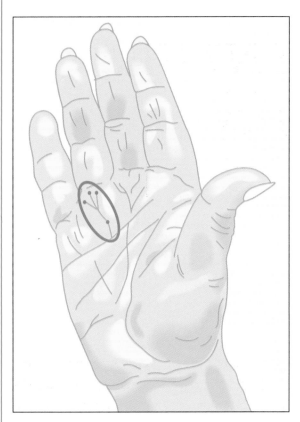

■ *Fig. VII.18. The trident lets us give a reasoned mental form to an abstract idea.*

The trident gives us the ability to give a rational form to abstract ideas, so that we can use them in our daily lives. It can rescue ancestral ideas and feelings from the depths of our subconscious and apply reason to confirm their existence.

The trident revolutionizes rusty or conventional ideas. Those who possess it will be able to put new ideas into practice with an understanding of what is right for their time. Depending on its location, the trident may be the sign of a healer, a psychologist, a psychiatrist, a priest or any professional whose aim is to reach a greater understanding of his fellow men in order to be able to help them.

CHAPTER VIII

THE ADVENTURE BEGINS

The first hint of curiosity launches us on the adventure of chirology, even though it may well seem that it is chirology which chooses us. After our first brush with it, however fleeting, we cannot forget it and we feel the urge to find out more. In fact, as we mentioned at the beginning, Man has an innate need to interpret everything he sees around him. That is why we find chirology so alluring.

You do not have to be out of the ordinary in order to develop your powers of prediction; anybody can do it. But you will never know what you are capable of until you try it, so let us begin and your hands will soon be an open book.

It is undeniable that you are taking on a great responsibility when we decide to read someone's hands. Your client will expect you to help, encourage and advise him, so you should never frighten or depress him with your reading. Before mentioning any distressing or worrying situation, you should remember that every problem has a solution. You must be sure that you have interpreted the matter correctly and be positive in your explanation of it. It is always better not to mention something if you are not sure of your interpretation, rather than terrify people for no good reason. Do not forget that a reading should lift people's spirits and not feed the nagging fears and doubts that torment us all. If you suffuse your reading with love you will be rewarded with wisdom.

GUIDELINES FOR A READING

It is a good idea to choose comfortable and relaxed surroundings with good lighting and to sit opposite your client without any obstacle in between to interfere with the flow of energy from one person to another (fig. VIII.1).

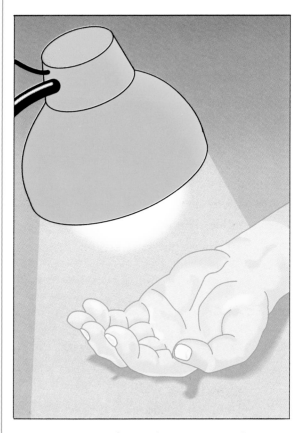

■ *Fig. VIII.1. When reading someone's palm it is a good idea to choose a comfortable place with good lighting.*

A chirologist should try to put his own worries aside and concentrate on his work. A useful tip is to create certain signals to mark the beginning and end of a reading. This prevents you from becoming too involved in your client's problems. These signals could be a prayer or a phrase that you repeat to yourself whenever you begin or end a session. You could also use fragrances or perfumes that you keep especially for this purpose. Your aim is to signal to your subconscious that you need concentration in order to carry out your task successfully and, for this, you can use any of your senses.

Next you will inspect the palm and back of both hands, noting their shape, colour, size, consistency and flexibility. Until you have gained experience it is advisable to consult your notes whenever necessary. If you have any doubts about the type of hand you have before you it is best to choose the closest likeness and give your reading accordingly. Remember that you should keep your reading simple; complicated comparisons will not make you a good palmist.

Next we will look at the most common types of hand.

Size

We have seen that if someone's hands are big in comparison with their body, this person will be conscientious, slow, thoughtful and frank (fig. VIII.2). If the hands are small, this person will take in a situation at a glance. He will make quick, precise appraisals but in his haste he may make mistakes (fig. VIII.3). A person with a balanced hand will be able to analyze in detail or get an overall impression of the situation, according to what is needed at the time (fig. VIII.4).

The wider the hand, the more generous, sociable, open and trusting its owner will be. A person with narrow hands will tend to be introverted and to place restrictions on himself and on others. However, he will have good powers of concentration. By looking at the size and width of the hands you will get your first indication of your client's character (fig. VIII.5).

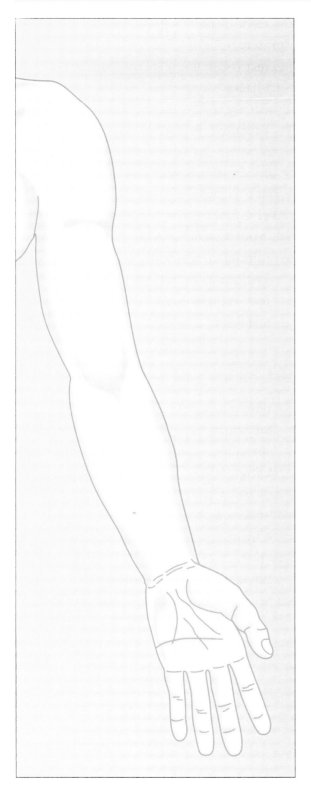

■ *Fig. VIII.2. The size of the hand must be judged in comparison with the arm, never on its own.*

Texture

If a person's skin is delicate and soft, they will be vulnerable to their surroundings. Their mind will be strong and their feelings will flow freely (fig. VIII.6). If it is dry, rough, hard and flaky, their health will not easily be affected by external factors. However, they will tend to express their feelings badly and repress them until they overwhelm them. Their mind will harbour fears and weaknesses which will show up as hard areas or callouses on their skin.

Consistency

If someone's hands feel flabby to the touch they will lack energy and willpower and tend to give up easily (fig. VIII.7).

Firm hands show energy, activity, strength and responsibility, but also difficulty in adapting to situations (fig. VIII.8).

If they are so hard that they hardly give at all when pressed, this person will take an excessively firm stance and adapt very badly. He retains his energy so much that he is prone to sudden fits of rage.

Flexibility

Flexible hands are a sign of people who are unpredictable in their actions and their feelings. They take orders and accept new ideas easily although they lack concentration and cannot do more than one thing at a time. An inflexible hand is cautious, responsible, stubborn and hard-working. This person has an inflexible character and difficulty in adapting to new ideas and situations. He likes secrets

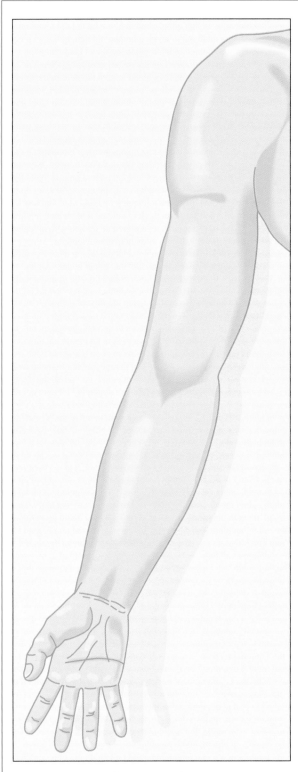

and keeps his feelings and his problems to himself.

Colour

White hands belong to calm, peace-loving people with great sex appeal and a tendency to be materialistic. Red hands (fig. VIII.10) belong to active, expansive, temperamental people who are also impatient, spirited, ambitious and irritable. Yellow hands (fig. VIII.11) reveal fanaticism, cunning, intelligence and a calculating and exacting nature.

Shape

A square hand is the sign of a methodical, orderly and practical person. He is good at making plans for others to carry out. A spatular hand indicates bold, self-confident people who work themselves to nervous exhaustion. They are the ideal people for carrying out the plans made by those with square hands. A conical hand denotes reason and intuition. These people are active, hard-working, independent and lovers of beauty. They may be either realistic or dreamers. Those with conical hands can judge and criticize the plans made by square hands and carried out by spatular hands.

If your client is a person with big, wide, square hands, soft skin with a reddish hue and inflexible joints you can deduct that he is a conscientious, slow, thoughtful, very sociable, open and trusting person. He has a strong mind and he expresses his feelings openly and courageously although his health is vulnerable to changes in the weather. He will be very temperamental, ambitious and hard-working but also inflexible and headstrong. He is particularly suited to jobs requiring method and calculation and his treatment of others is honest and fair. In a matter of minutes you can gather enough information to give you a fairly complete and reliable picture of your client's character.

This initial character sketch should encourage you to look deeper and begin a more detailed analysis. Beginning with the nails (fig. VIII.12), remember that a reddish tone shows a tendency to suffer from high blood pressure, over-excitement and fits of anger. Those with blue nails will have bad circulation and will repress their emotions in front of others, appearing cold.

A yellow tinge suggests liver problems and constipation. These people feel overwhelmed by problems that they do not know how to solve. Very pale nails denote poor health and a resentful nature. Short nails belong to argumentative, critical, impatient people whilst wide nails denote anger but without malice. Long, narrow nails belong to people with bad tempers who are easily frustrated. Those with almond shaped nails are generous and capable of sacrificing themselves for others, whilst clawed nails are a sign of the coward or miser.

Whilst you examine the nails and gather information to add to your client's psychological profile you must bear in mind what finger each nail belongs to and what hand it is on. Any difference in the nails on the left and right hands will lead to a modification in the meaning of that particular nail (whether for better or for worse) and will affect your client's future.

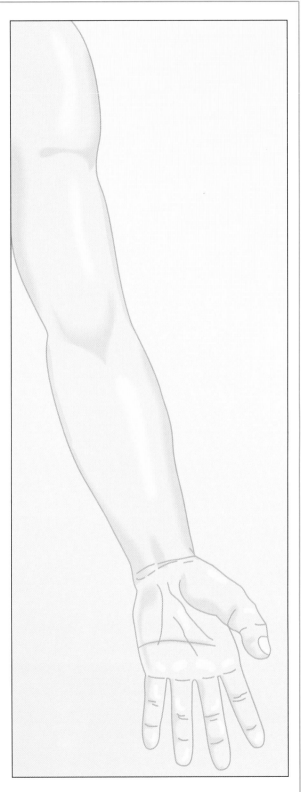

■ *Fig. VIII.4. A hand in keeping with the body shows a capacity for analysis.*

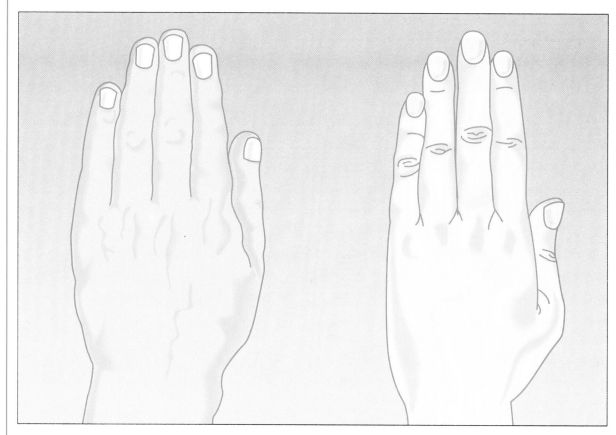

■ *Fig. VIII.5. It is advisable to look at the back of the hand in order to judge its width.*

THE IMPORTANCE OF THE FINGERS

You can glean so much vital information from the fingers that they merit special attention. You know that each finger has its own personality (fig. VIII.13) so now you can be more specific in your reading.

The index finger reflects your character: ambition, pride, honour, devotion and anger.

The middle finger separates reality from imagination and provides us with prudence, wisdom, pessimism, fatalism and melancholy.

The ring finger shows your involvement with other people and provides us with love, joy, success, artistry, resourcefulness, and cheerfulness.

The little finger is the smart one and rules over diplomacy, commerce, science and sexuality.

The thumb reasserts your human qualities, giving rise to your emotions, willpower, logic and reason.

In your analysis of the fingers you should note their structure, their flexibility, the joints and the distance between them, the shape of their tips, their straightness and their base.

You must always compare each finger with its equivalent on the other hand and note any differences.

Base

The greater the gap between two fingers the more independent that person will be in the facets of his character ruled by those fingers.

In general, fingers which are close together indicate reserve, caution, excessive worry and a tendency to hoard things (fig. VIII.14). A big gap indicates confidence, independence and an ability to communicate (fig. VIII.15). Here is what each gap means:

A gap between the index and middle fingers means an independent way of thinking.

A gap between the middle and ring fingers means independence from external factors.

A gap between the ring and little fingers means independence in your behaviour.

The gap between the index finger and thumb shows your degree of total independence.

When one finger begins lower down than the others there will be inferiority complexes related to the qualities which you attribute to that finger. However, if all the fingers begin on a level it indicates a dangerous excess of self-confidence.

Structure

Long fingers denote people who are meticulous and pay attention to detail. Short fingers show a tendency to pleasure and sensuous enjoyment but they do not exclude feeling. Slender fingers show sensitivity and refine-

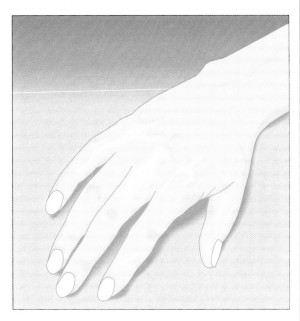

■ *Fig. VIII.6. A delicate hand shows a strong psyche.*

ment and express emotions well. Bear in mind that there may be long and short, fat and thin fingers on the same hand and that while the index finger on one hand may be short it may be long on the other hand. These discrepancies could be the key to traumas and sufferings lived through in the past or awaiting us in the future.

Phalanxes

In a previous chapter we have seen how each phalanx has a unique capacity which can be used to solve problems. If you notice that one phalanx is redder or more lined than the others you will have discovered which capacity your client finds it hardest to use. You can also find out which capacities are most useful to him. Beginning with the phalanxes furthest from the palm you have:

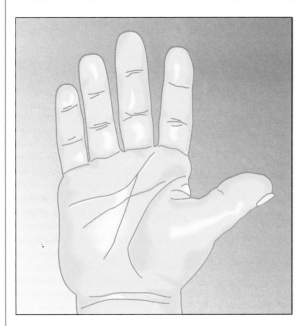

■ *Fig. VIII.7. A flabby hand shows a lack of will-power and energy, in the absence of indications to the contrary.*

Index finger - Individuality, fecundity and persuasion.

Middle finger - Reality, reasoning and spontaneity.

Ring finger - Desires, drive and self-denial.

Little finger - Harmony, deep emotions and the balance between feminine and masculine.

Since everything the palm receives and sends out passes through the fingers, the phalanxes act as filters which purify in-going and out-going ideas. That is why the degree of flexibility you have in your fingers is so important and, above all, the shape of your fingertips since they are the point of entry and exit.

The pointed fingertip, also known as the intuitive fingertip, gives you the ability to think fast. The spatular fingertip or active fingertip gives you a capacity for work and the square or organised fingertip gives you balance and good visual perception.

It is a good idea to examine the knuckles, the hair on the back of the hand and the point of origin of the fingers on both sides of the hand. You should note whether the fingers are straight or bent since the latter indicates that the person in question is not very sure of that finger's personality and seeks the protection of the finger next to it.

The final step in the analysis of the fingers is to look at both thumbs and make a mental note of any differences between the two. Remember that when the phalanx nearest to the palm is flexible you will be generous with material things and will not worry about your financial security. When the other phalanx is flexible your generosity will be psychological

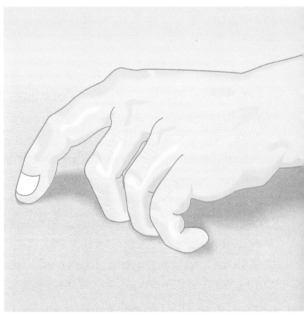

■ *Fig. VIII.8. A firm hand is strong, energetic and responsible.*

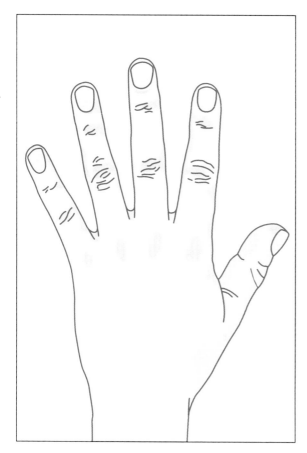

■ *Fig. VIII.9. White hands convey tranquility, calm and sex-appeal.*

Once you have determined the meaning of all this information you will have a fairly reliable psychological profile of your client which you can add to throughout the reading.

It would be a sorry mistake not to make use of the feelings you experience during the session, or not to pay attention to the feel of your client's hand. The mere gathering of information without intuition will result in an accurate but unfeeling interpretation. It is important to feel the hand constantly until you get used to its messages.

Once you have completed this initial analysis you should inform your client as clearly as possible of your findings. You should aim to

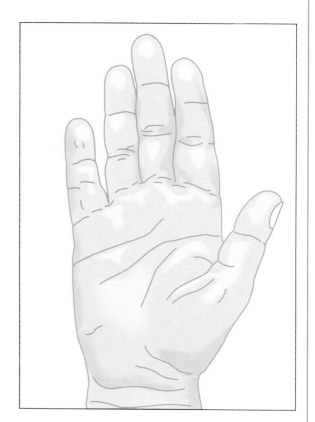

■ *Fig. VIII.10. Red hands are impatient, ambitious and full of fight. In their work they have both qualities and defects.*

and emotional and you will always be ready to help others.

You must not forget to look at the back of the hands to see the rotation of the thumbs. When the thumb faces the same way as the fingers so that all the nails can be seen at the same time, it shows an inability to withstand temptation and a tendency to be easily led.

When the thumb is at right angles to the fingers and a third of the nail can be seen it is a sign of self-control; you want to be in control of your actions, not from any feelings of guilt but out of self respect.

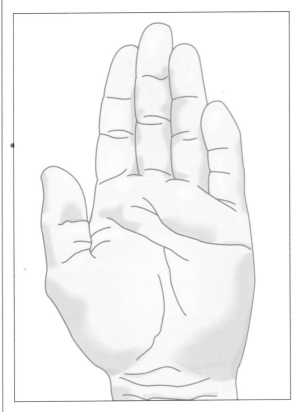

■ *Fig. VIII.11. Yellow hands indicate fanaticism, cunning and a calculating nature.*

pay special attention to his virtues in order to give him a positive picture of himself, even though you are aware that behind every virtue there lurks a fault. However, it would not be a good idea to begin a reading with a depressing list of deficiencies. You should also aim not to stay silent for long since that could unnerve your client and make him think you have seen something unpleasant.

ANALYSIS OF THE MOUNTS

Next you will observe the size and quality of the mounts or fleshy pads. As is your custom you will compare the left and right hands,

detecting the energy each mount had and what use is being made of it at present. Note the shape of the karate chop and whether any mounts are absent or joined together, as these details have a meaning of their own. Let us go over the meanings of the mounts:

> High mount: abundance of qualities.
> Normal mount: existence of qualities.
> Low mount: inadequate qualities.
> Firm mount: energetic use of qualities.
> Soft mount: poor use of qualities.
> Mounts joined together: merging of respective qualities.

You must keep in mind the qualities related to each mount so that you can refer to them when your client has a problem you want to help him with (fig. VIII.17).

The qualities of Venus

This Mount reveals your capacity to love and be loved, your vitality, warmth and energy. It reveals your general state of health and, in particular, the health of your reproductive organs, kidneys, throat and ear. On the negative side it can lead to brutality, physical passion, and sensual or sexual appetites. Everything related to your family and children is located in this mount.

The qualities of Jupiter

Jupiter represents your growth as an individual. When it is in keeping with the other mounts it represents justice, a positive outlook on life, idealism, self-confidence and a

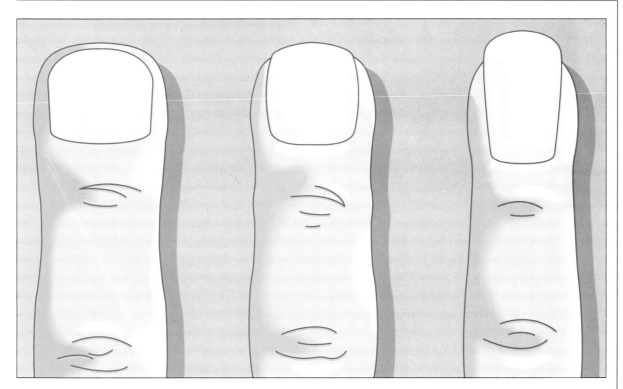

■ *Fig. VIII.12. The colour of the nails is a good way of diagnosing illnesses.*

desire to help others. On the other hand, it is also the mount of ambition, pride, vanity and selfishness together with a tendency to be domineering.

The qualities of Saturn

Saturn seeks to balance your personality. It allows you to even out the levels of idealism and reason in your development. It represents responsibility, self-preservation, the search for truth within oneself and your love of independence and of solitude. But it can also lead to fears, superstition, sadness, melancholy and excessive analysis and inflexibility.

The qualities of Apollo

Apollo represents a profound love of beauty, great creativity and great possibilities of honour and fame. But it also leads to vanity, self-indulgence, a love of luxury, extravagance and materialism.

The qualities of Mercury

This is the mount of commerce, writing, diplomacy and sexuality. When accompanied by a long little finger it indicates a talent for public speaking and business. However, when it is covered in a tangle of lines it may be a

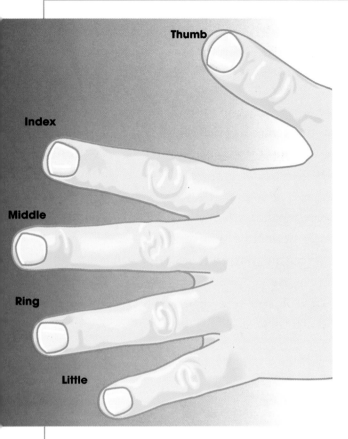

■ *Fig. VIII.13. The thumb confirms your human condition. The index finger shows the personality you have developed. The middle finger shows the balance in that personality. The ring finger shows your public side and the little finger your cunning and diplomacy.*

The qualities of active Mars

Mars represents aggression and life's daily struggle. Its weapons are ingenuity, which it receives from Mercury just above it, and intuition, which it receives from the Moon below it.

The qualities of passive Mars

This represents courage and resistance to the manipulations of others. It shows if you have been hurt, if you are resigned, or afraid, or if your emotions are about to overwhelm us. The protective shields of Mars are justice and pri-

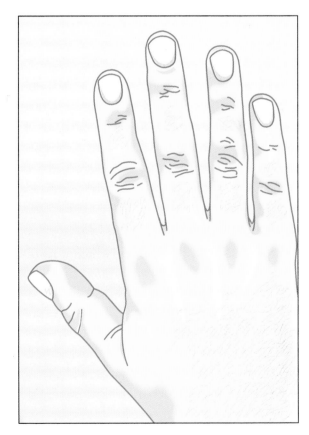

■ *Fig. VIII.14. A small gap between fingers may indicate an excessive dependence on others.*

sign of robbery, deceit, undesirable sexual inclinations and even, a criminal mind.

The qualities of the Moon

This is home to your subconscious impressions and impulses, your instincts and imagination. It reveals an interest in religion, mysticism and in extrasensory perception.

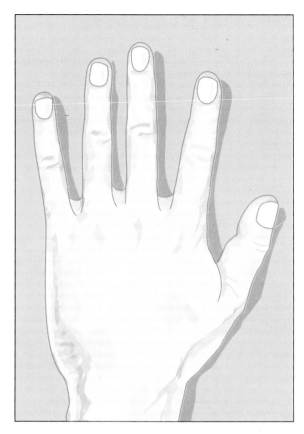

■ *Fig. VIII.15. A big gap between fingers indicates independence and a capacity for communicating.*

must be consulted when analyzing any mount, finger, line, or phalanx.

Now you will begin to study the lines. Do not forget about the three bracelets on the wrist which summarize man's three driving forces. Remember that they begin beneath the left thumb and end beneath the right thumb. The one closest to the palm is the first and is related to your health. Just below it is the second parallel line tracing the changes in your finances and, finally, the third one (almost on your arm), which indicates how much love you give and receive. The absence of one of these lines does not show any weakness in these areas, but merely indicates that

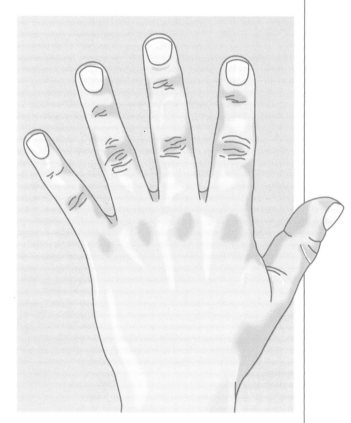

■ *Fig. VIII.16. The back of the hand and the knuckles give some indication of that person's way of thinking.*

de, which it receives from Jupiter above it, and the pleasures of the senses, which it receives from Venus below it.

The qualities of the Valley of Neptune

This valley reveals your present work situation and how you feel about it. It indicates your capacity for influencing others, for public speaking, and for healing people.

You must never forget to read both hands at the same time in order to see both the active and passive side of an event. Both hands

your energy flows through different channels. These lines are like the index of a book which is there for consultation throughout the reading. However, it is important to compare them at the start in order to get an idea of the past and future in these three chapters of life.

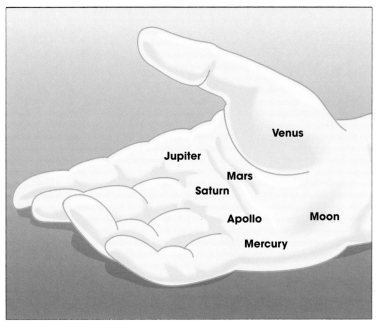

■ *Fig. VIII.17. Each mount or fleshy pad on the palm corresponds to a particular facet of your character.*

THE THREE MOTHER LINES

If you said that the bracelets are the index of your book, then the heart, head and life lines (also known as Mother lines) are the three chapters you should read (fig. VIII.18). To find out what these chapters are about and whether one is more important than the others it is necessary to compare the lines on both hands. If the life line is the clearest and forms a broad curve you will be ambitious, full of vitality, resistant to illness and of strong constitution. If it begins high up near the index finger your tenacity and ambition will be greater. A break in the life line marks a complete change in your way of life and any ragged area implies a lack of strength or faltering courage. The length of your life line shows

how intensely you will live, not how long.

When the strongest line is the head line you have great concentration, self-esteem, self-control and a strong psyche. If it begins together with the life line you will not develop your initiative and become independent until the two lines separate. However, if the head line is separate from the start you are rasher, more restless and independent. As in the previous case, if the line is short, your thought processes are quicker and more intense, but if it is long they are more moderate and organized. Always check on where the line starts, the route it takes and where it points to.

A clear heart line which stands out from the others reveals a person with a strong heart who is generous, warm, affectionate, idealistic and faithful in love. The closer to the fingers the line begins, the more warm and affectionate the person is, whilst the lower down it begins (close to the head line), the colder the person will seem. The presence of islands on this line indicates doubts and barren periods in his or her affections. Dark spots may predict heart diseases.

Once you have compared these three lines you can begin your reading. You should start with the life line on the left hand and analyze the experiences from the beginning (which marks the moment of birth) to the end, taking it centimetre by

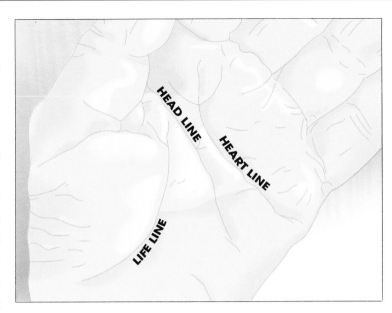

■ *Fig. VIII.18. The three main lines.*

centimetre. You should check the effect that these experiences have had on the head and heart lines. The purpose of reading the past is not to show how much you know or to impress others with your skill but to find out how your client's mind works in order to advise him correctly when you begin the reading of the right hand. Above all, you need to find out how time is measured on your client's hand and be able to judge the distance between two major events in his life, otherwise you will not be capable of interpreting his projects for the future.

As I have said several times already, a palmist does not guess at the future so you should not be afraid to ask for information when you are not sure of your interpretation. It is vital to explain the basis of your work to your client so that their silence (sometimes a desire not to disturb your concentration) does not lead you

to false conclusions. A successful reading benefits you both but depends on the rapport you manage to establish.

At this stage in the reading you should feel confident enough to apply the general concepts you have learnt, keeping all the meanings in mind. Your great ally is colour, both in the line and around it. For example, if the beginning of the life line is dark in colour it could signify a problematic birth but if the surrounding is white it means that your relatives, and in particular your parents, welcomed you with love. A small square on this line indicates a change of address, whilst an island means health problems or a time of physical weakness. You must follow this line, step by step, stopping each time you reach a sign, a division or a change in colour which is trying to tell you that something important has happened in this person's life. Consequently, you should focus all your attention on this event as if you were watching it unfold before your eyes and as if the hand were only trying to tell you about that one event.

The lines, symbols and colours are the actors who act out the script you are working

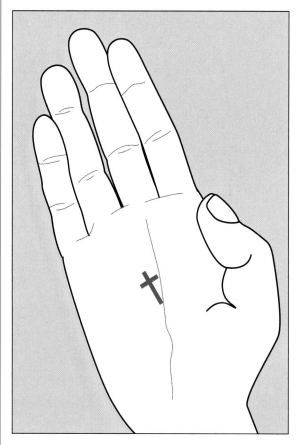

■ *Fig. VIII.19. A cross on the fate line marks an event which will force you to evaluate your career.*

on, and the mounts are the backdrops to your play. If you could manage to view each experience as though it were a scene of the play being acted out before you, you would forget about past and future and see only the scenes unfolding before us, with the same backdrops but different scripts, the same actors but cast in different roles. This is the secret of a good reading; to use all the hand, either to interpret a single event or to see a summary of your client's whole life.

SYMBOLS

Bearing in mind that the signs which are going to punctuate the most important events in our lives are the symbols that you saw in chapter VII, let us briefly go over their meanings according to their position on the hand.

The cross

A cross on the life line can be interpreted as a minor illness, an accident, a birth or a minor surgical operation. These events may befall the bearer of the sign or any close relative.

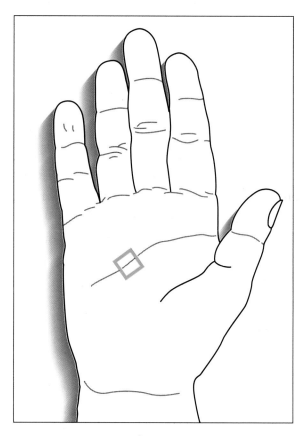

■ *Fig. VIII.20. A square on the head line may mean worries related to your house. This sign, wherever it may appear, is a protective sign.*

On the head line it signifies an important event which you are forced to resolve in your mind without delay.

On the heart line it indicates the complete or partial breakdown of a love affair.

On the fate line (fig. VIII.19) it marks the end of a job or a minor failure in your studies. In some cases it can signify that a colleague falls ill or retires and that you can be affected by this for better or for worse.

The square

On the life line it means a change of house or job (above all, if the person in question has been in the same place for a long time).

On the head line (fig. VIII.20) it can indicate an obsession with the payment of a house or problems with a legal document. A double square may refer to something you have read which has made a big impression on you or to a book that you want to write.

When a perfectly formed square is located on the heart line it represents a house in which you will make your home and be happy.

On the fate line it may mean that you set up your own business or that there is a change for the better in your job.

The triangle

A triangle on the life line means that you have learnt or are learning from your experiences. It can also mean that you have considerably improved your relations with others (you have improved your social skills).

On the heart line (fig. VIII.21) it shows that some situation or someone you like is tea-

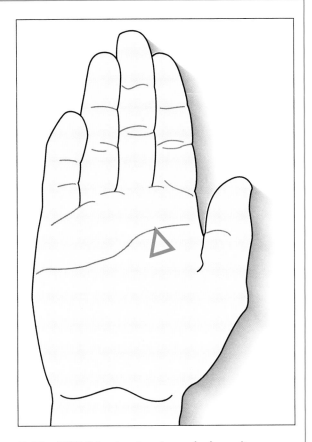

■ *Fig. VIII.21. A triangle on the heart line means that you are learning to love.*

ching you the meaning of commitment, love and affection.

On the head line it reveals enrichment as the result of an inner search for truth. You have got to know yourself better.

On the fate line it may refer to studies which will further your career. If the inside of the triangle is very white it may mean an unexpected windfall.

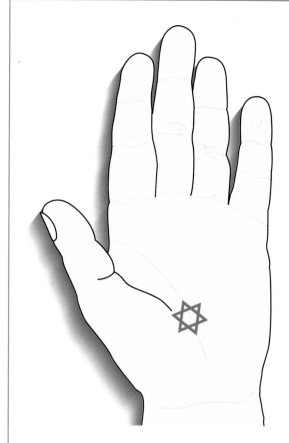

■ *Fig. VIII.22. A star on the life line brings good luck, especially if it is at the beginning.*

The star

A star on the life line (fig. VIII.22) is a sign of good luck. You will be surrounded by danger but, fortunately, you will always triumph over it.

On the heart line it refers to a society of an altruistic or spiritual order which you will join or which will help you.

On the head line it is a dangerous sign since it may refer to a personality disorder and even to madness. It goes without saying that you should not make such a terrible prediction on the basis of a single sign but should look at the whole hand in search of other signs which could alleviate its meaning.

On the fate line it shows a profit-making society that you will work for or which you will set up in partnership.

The presence of chains on any of the lines indicates that you are slaves to an idea, person or object. An island shows that a certain

problem is holding you up and you must solve it if you want to get on with life. When you are faced with an island it is very difficult to say what decision your client will finally make since the situation always involves serious doubts with no easy solution.

FINAL THOUGHTS

One way of working is to be guided by a single line, but you cannot ignore the messages of the minor lines when they appear, especially the fate line. This line begins near the wrist and is read upwards towards the fingers. All the signs, branches and changes in colour that you come across are trying to draw your attention to deviations, successes or conflicts in your work life. You should explore all the lines patiently, bearing in mind that some are more reliable than others. For example, the most practical minor lines are the fate line and the lines related to family, children and relationships. The rest are less reliable because they are not specific enough and, besides, they are difficult to recognize at first.

Once you have commented on the most important moments in your client's life you should sum up your findings and analyze his triumphs and failures. This is a good opportunity to confirm your first outline of his greatest virtues and defects. From this moment on the full weight of responsibility for the reading falls on your shoulders, since you will no longer have your client's help. This is where you begin your reading of the right hand. Nevertheless, the left hand will continue to guide you because the questions that you left unsolved in the past will come up time and time again in the future until you solve them.

You will read the right hand in the same way as you read the left. However, as you will be talking about the future this time, you must make it quite clear to your client that he is master of his own future, since the decisions he makes now will inevitably affect future events.

Furthermore, his hand will not show just one future, but several possibilities. You will explain them all to him so that he can choose the one that pleases him most, but at the same time you will try to explain the price he will have to pay for choosing that particular road.

You must try your hardest to discover in what areas of life your clients need to find harmony in order to reach their goals. You must advise them objectively without allowing your own beliefs or interests to interfere. In any case, it is always enriching to listen to the opinions of someone who is not involved in your problems, and you may even come to realize that your problems are shared by the greater part of mankind.

LIST OF ILLUSTRATIONS